Triads

of the

Major Scale

on Guitar

Copyright © 2018 Alexander Badiarov

- https://www.youtube.com/c/jazzguitartranscriptions
- https://www.instagram.com/panzerschwein

PayPal: elexandor@gmx.net // BUSD (BEP20): 0xEd979ad7E9d7E3f6f7cB7c2830aA2ae1DfBB1A6D

panzerschwein@gmx.de // Cologne, Germany

Feb 2022

~ Table Of Contents ~

Triads of the C major scale 1

Triads of the G major scale 17

Triads of the D major scale 33

Triads of the A major scale 49

Triads of the E major scale 65

Triads of the B major scale 81

Triads of the G^b major scale 97

Triads of the D^b major scale 113

Triads of the A^b major scale 129

Triads of the E^b major scale 145

Triads of the B^b major scale 161

Triads of the F major scale 177

Root Position (open voiced)

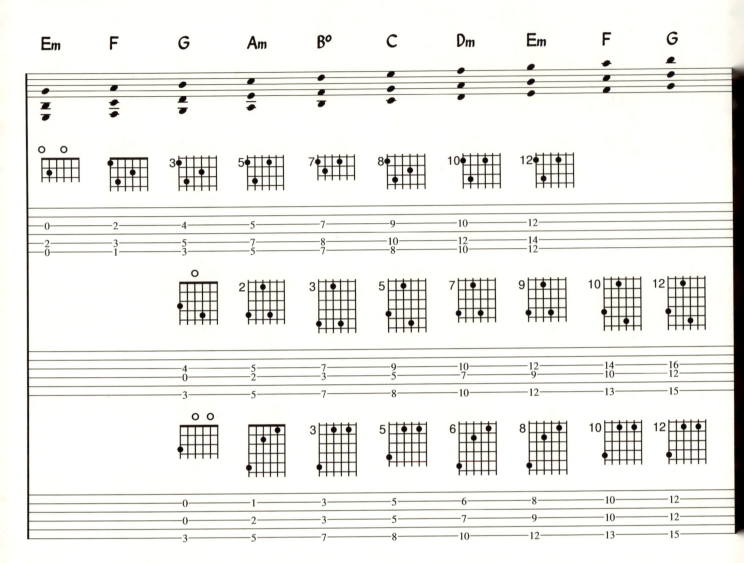

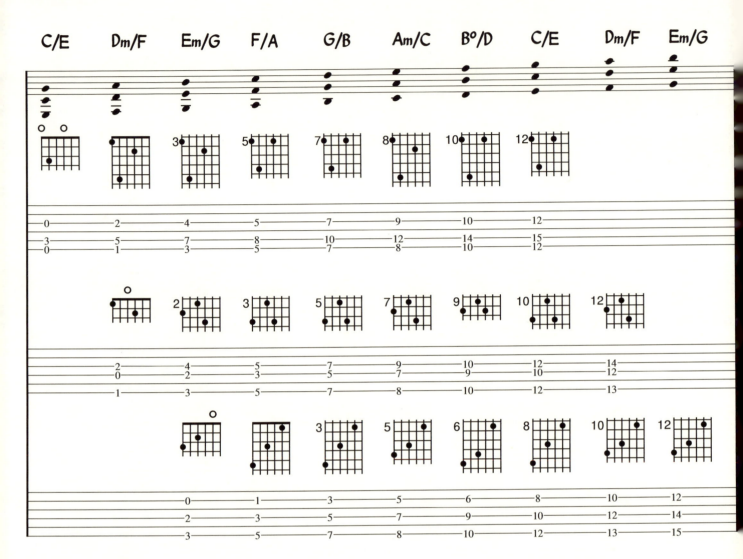

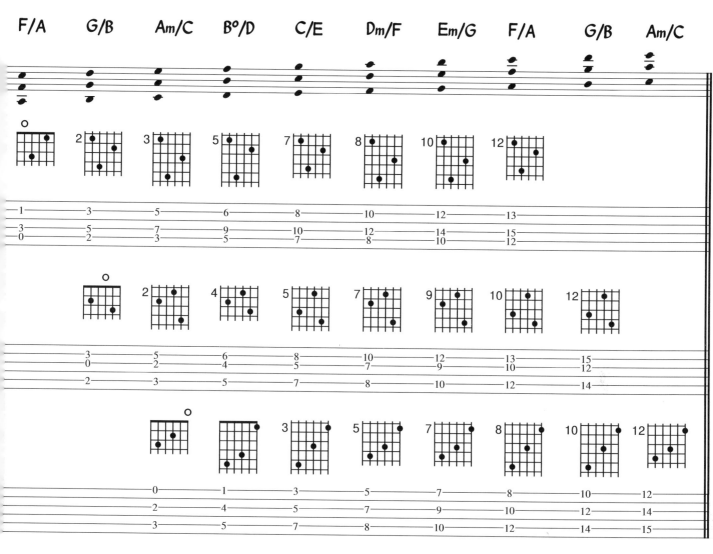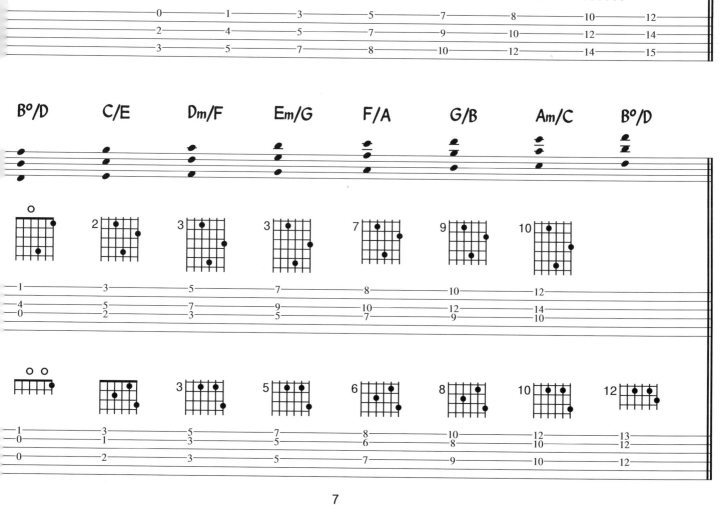

2nd inv. (open voiced)

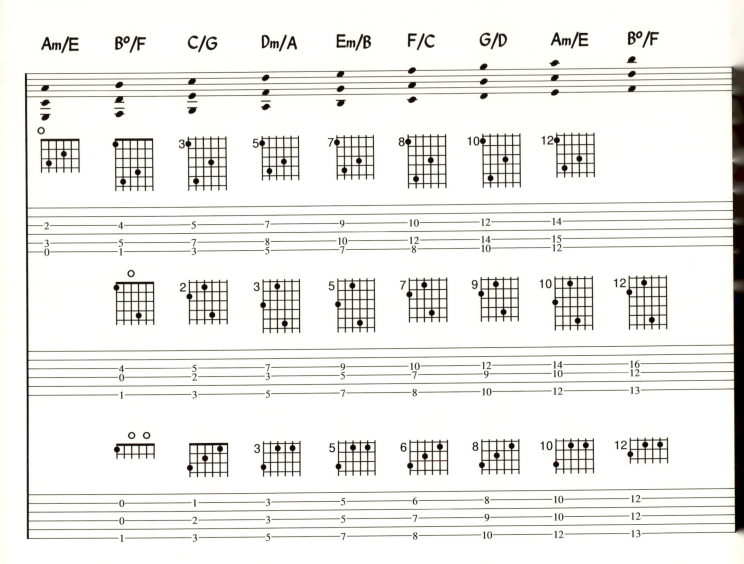

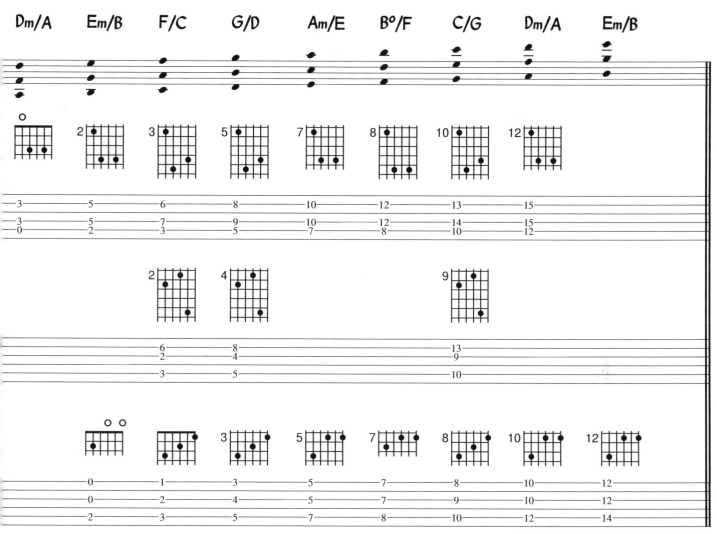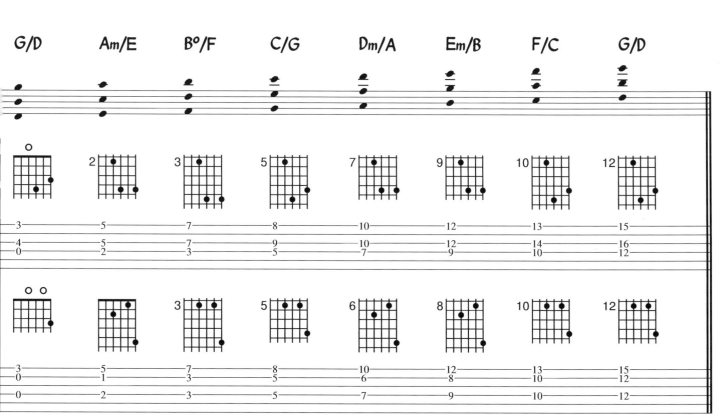

Root Position (open voiced, Version 2)

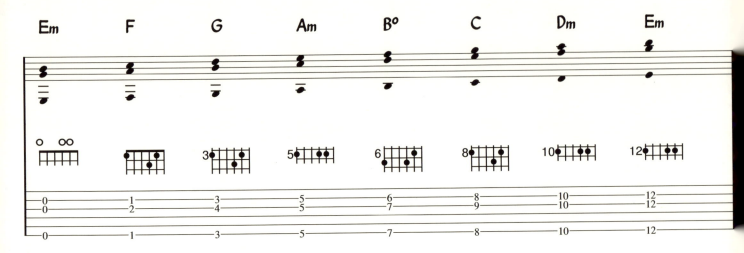
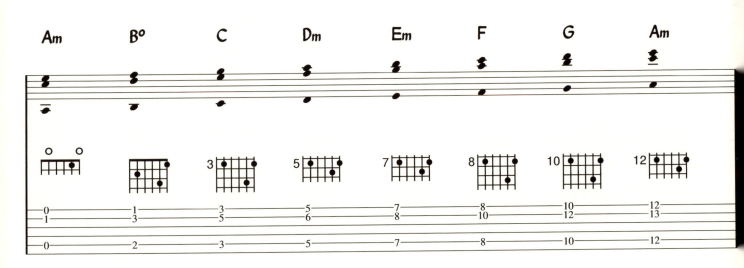

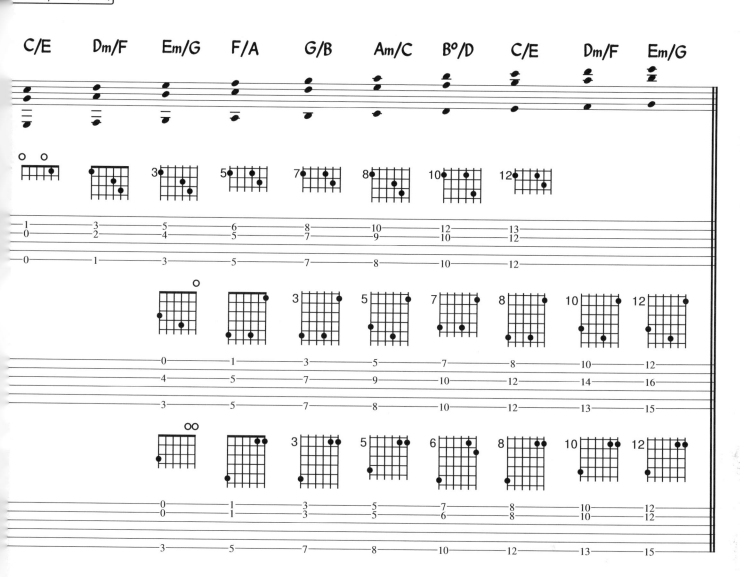
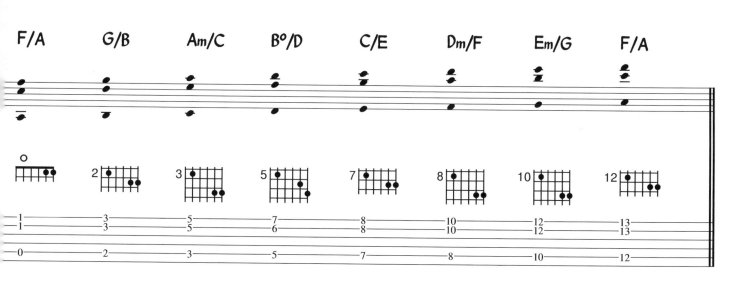

2nd inv. (open voiced, Version 2)

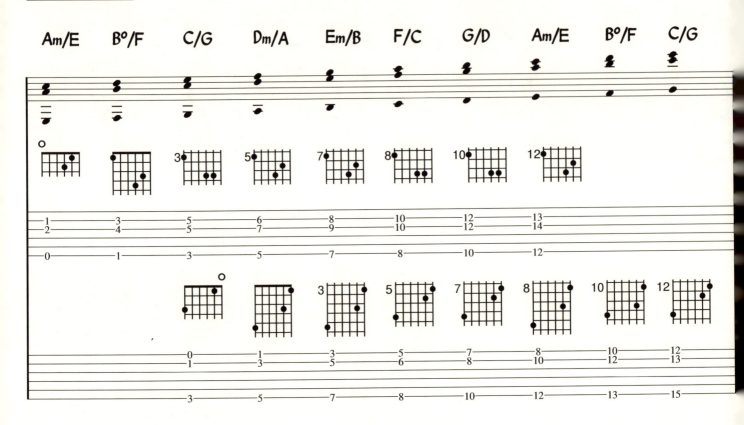

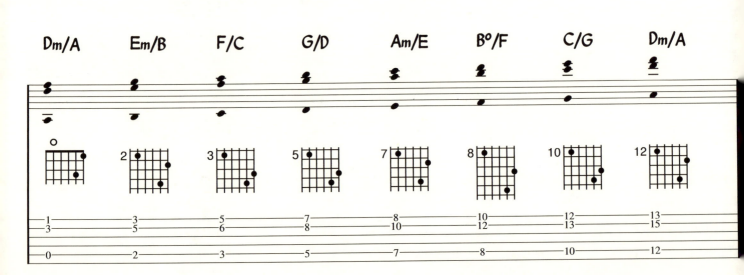

12

Root Position (open voiced, Version 3)

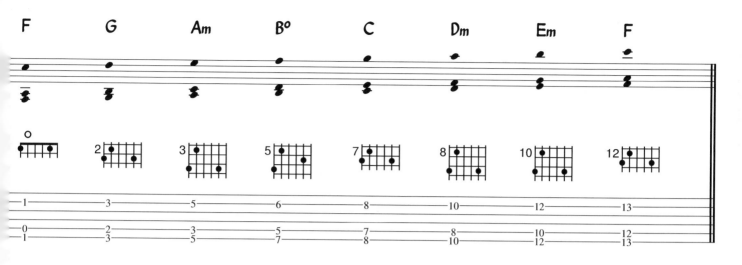

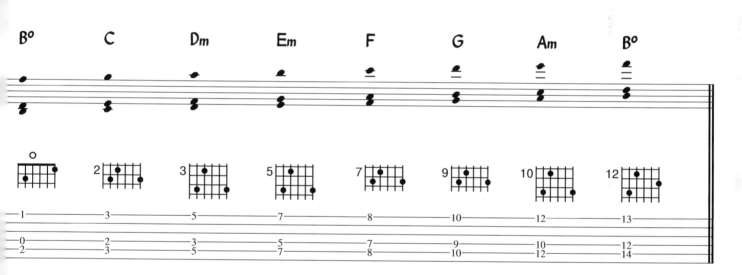

1st inv. (open voiced, Version 3)

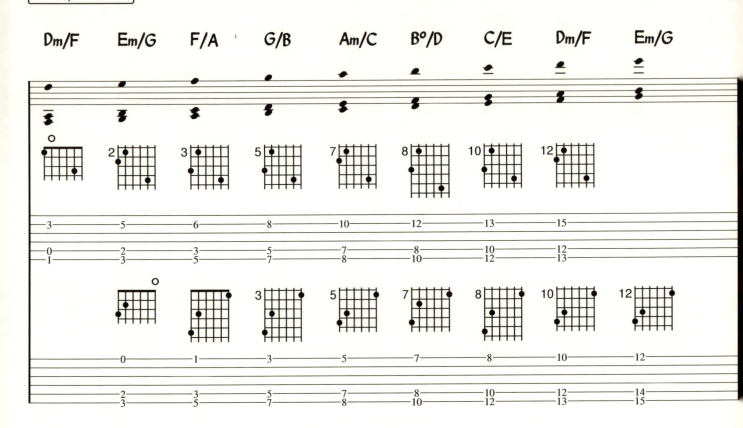

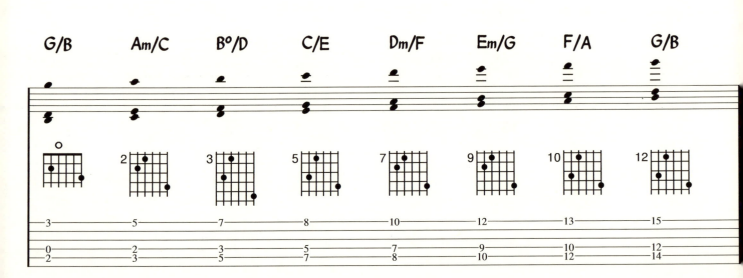

2nd inv. (open voiced, Version 3)

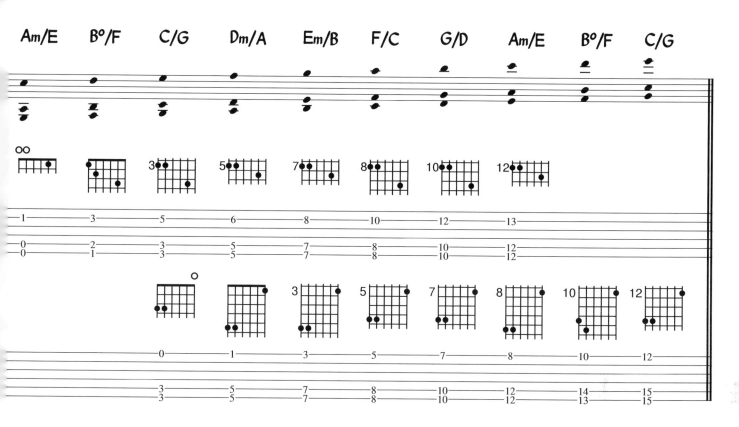

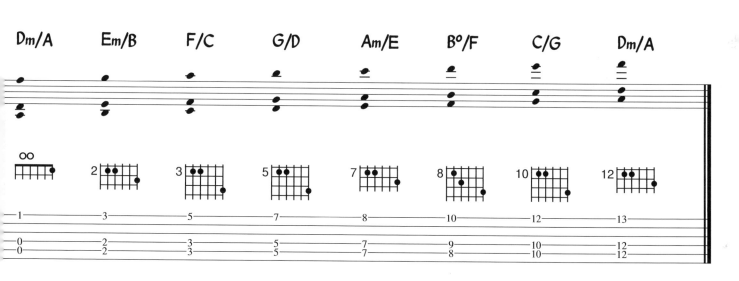

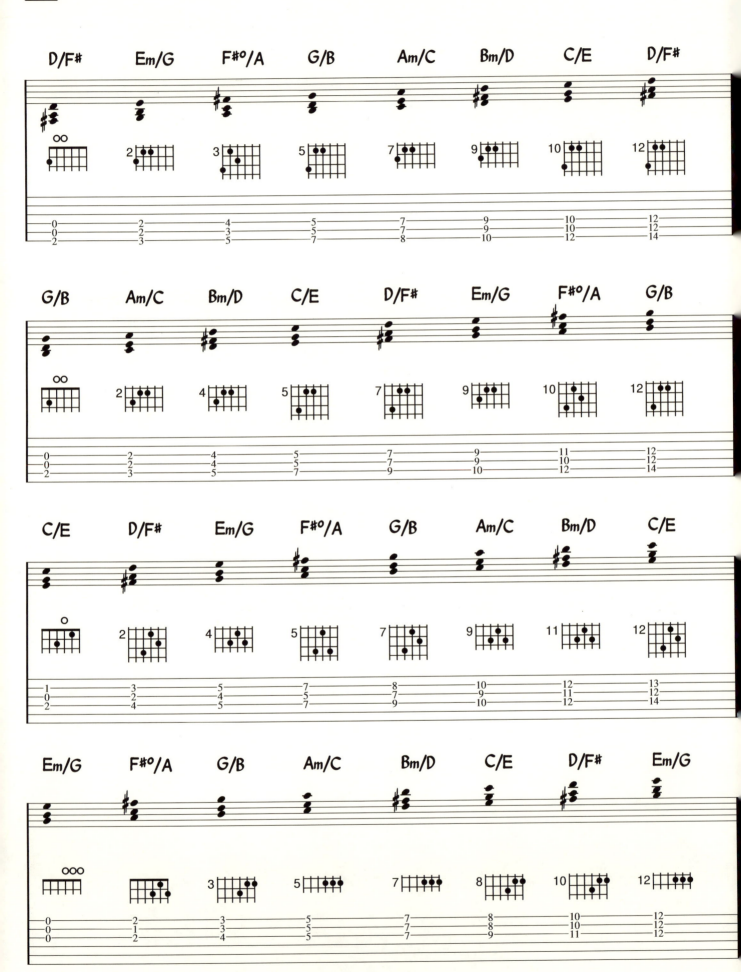

Root Position (open voiced)

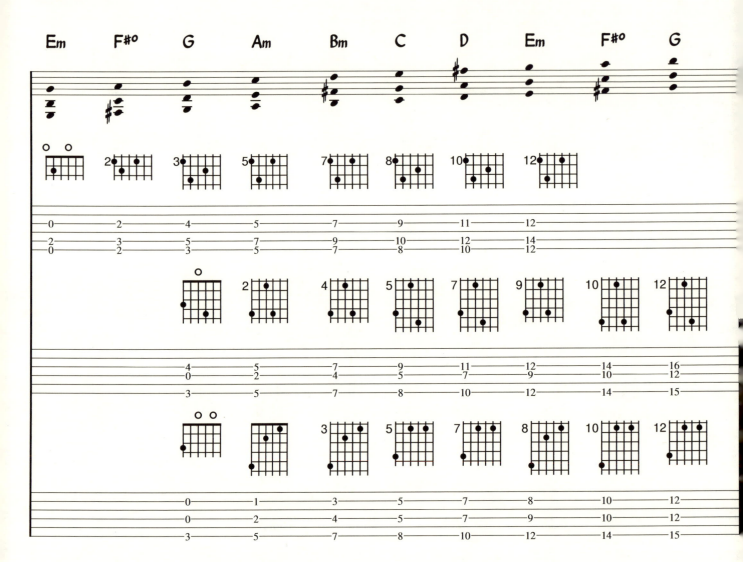

1st inv. (open voiced)

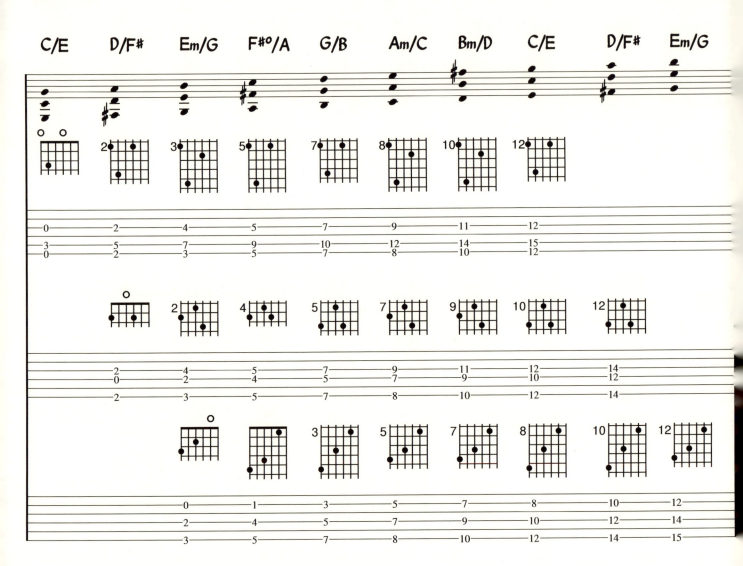

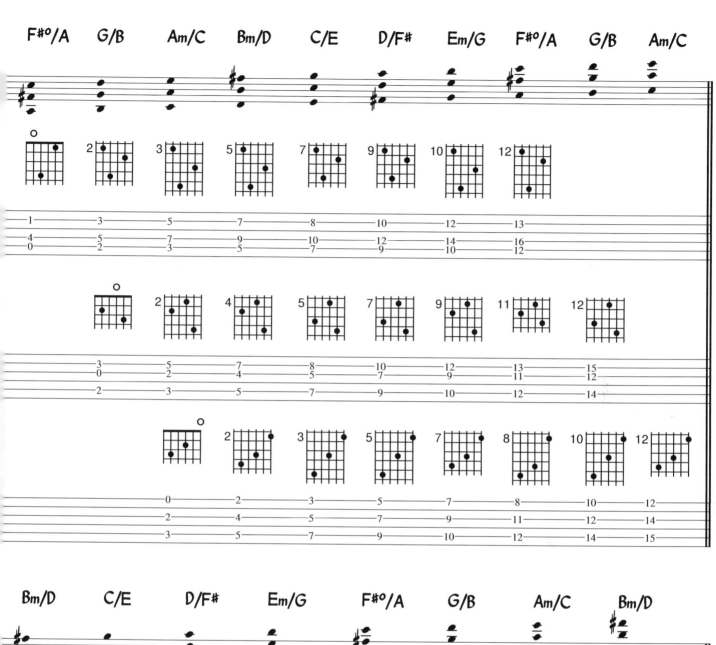
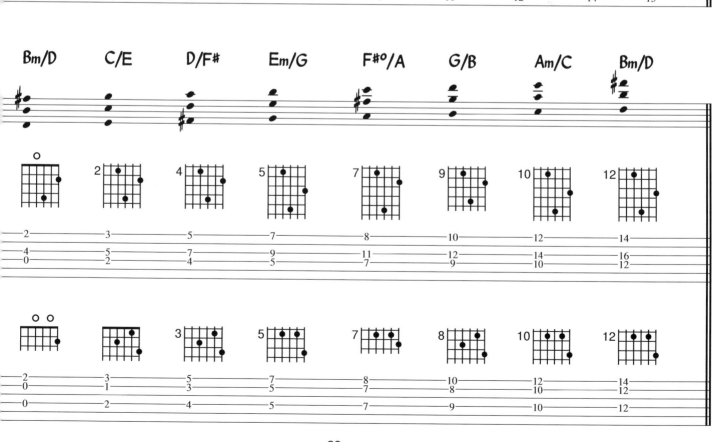

2nd inv. (open voiced)

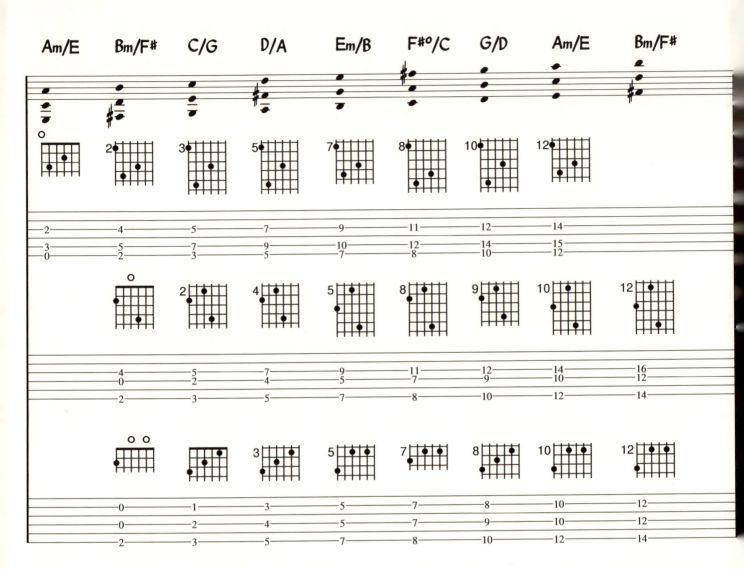

Root Position (open voiced, Version 2)

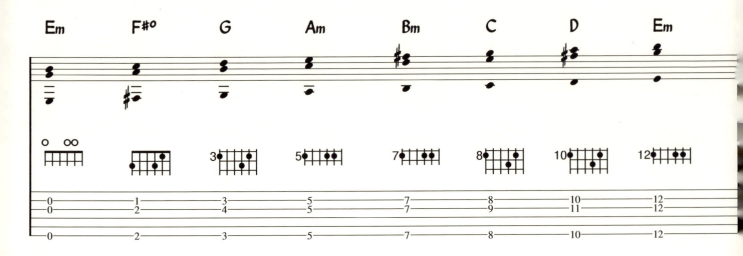
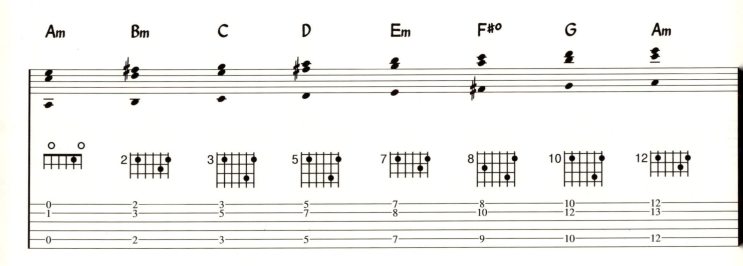

st inv. (open voiced, Version 2)

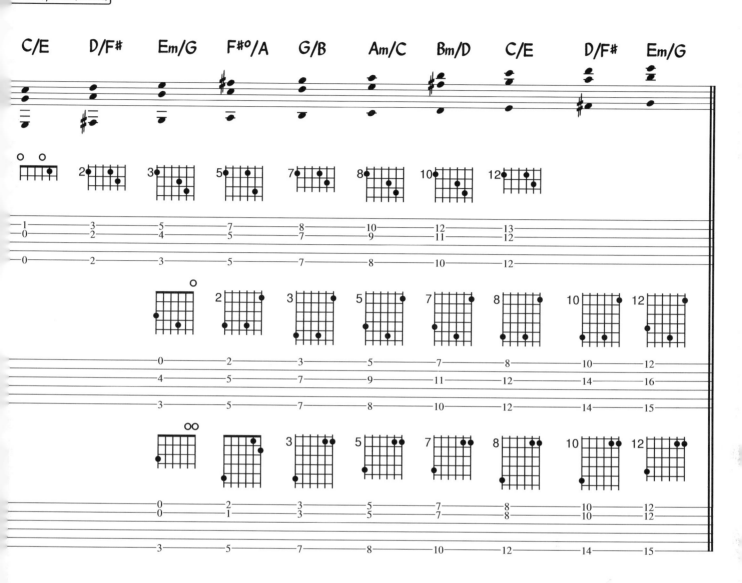
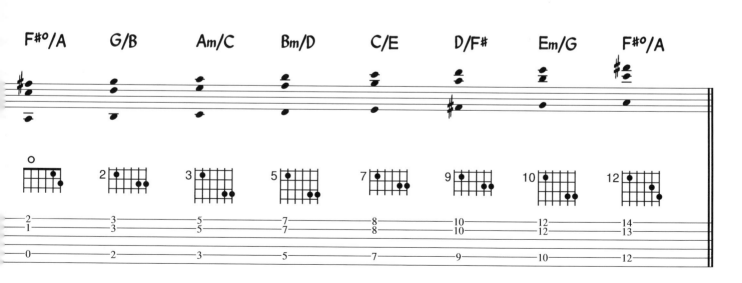

2nd inv. (open voiced, Version 2)

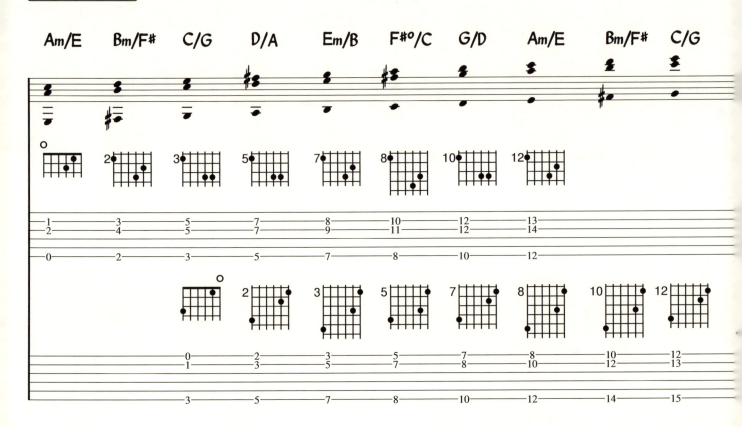

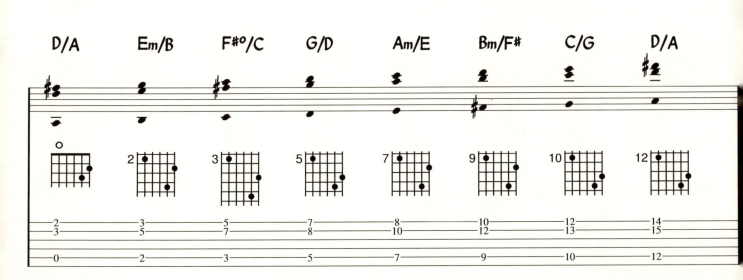

Root Position (open voiced, Version 3)

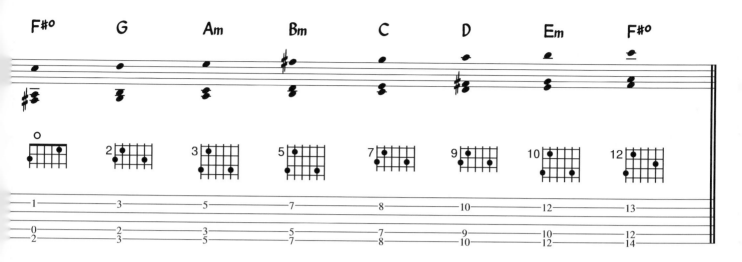
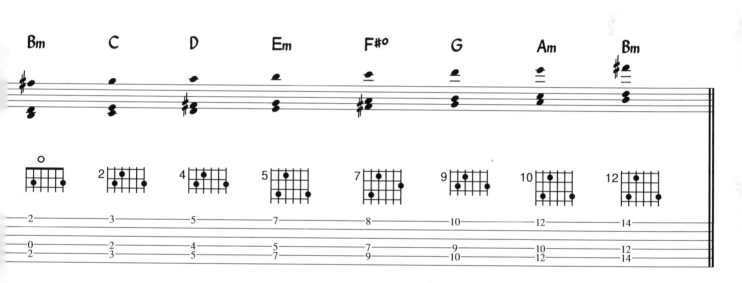

1st inv. (open voiced, Version 3)

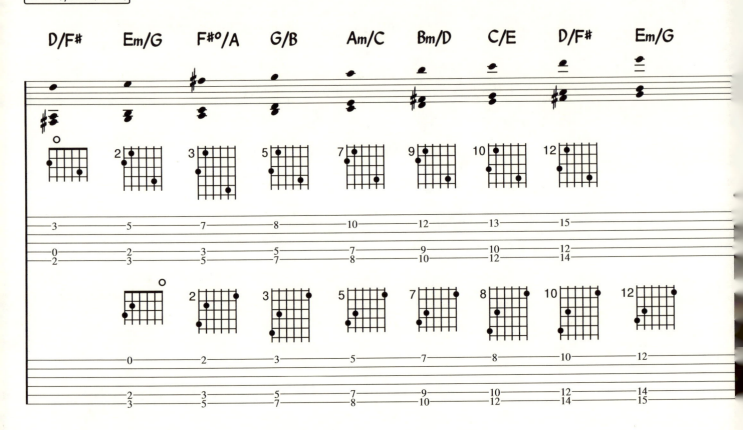
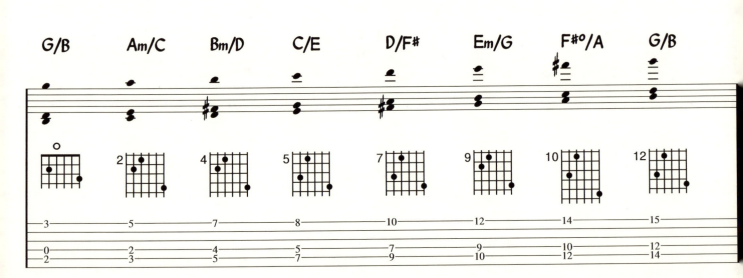

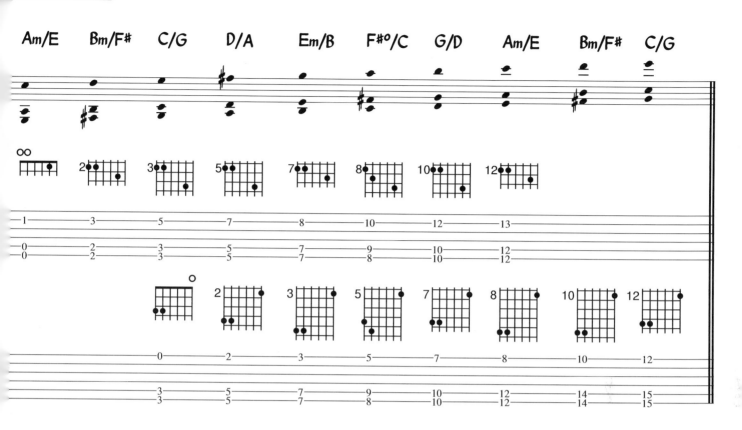
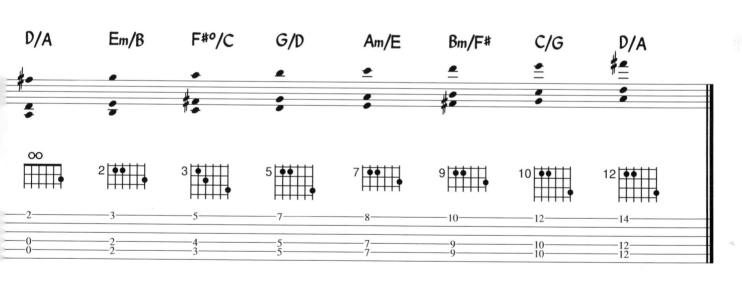

Root Position (open voiced)

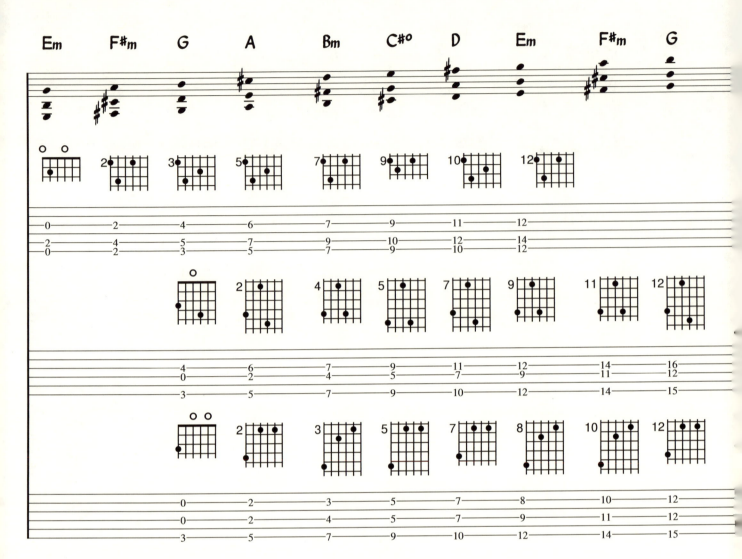

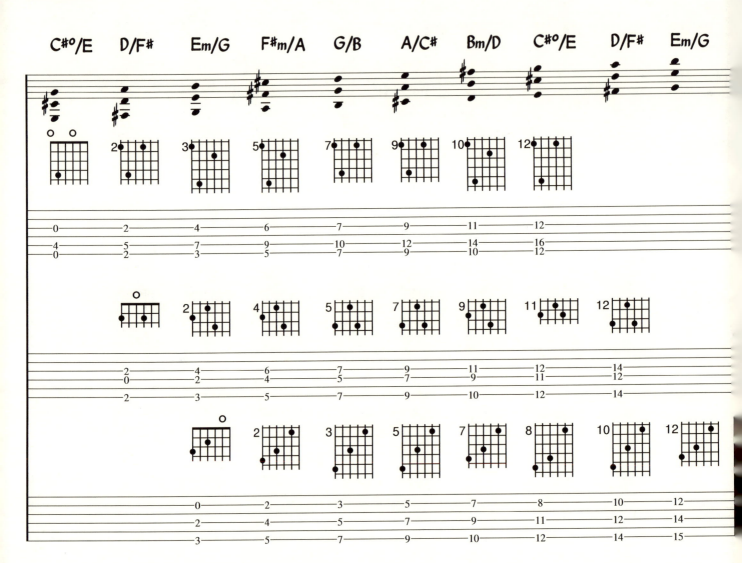

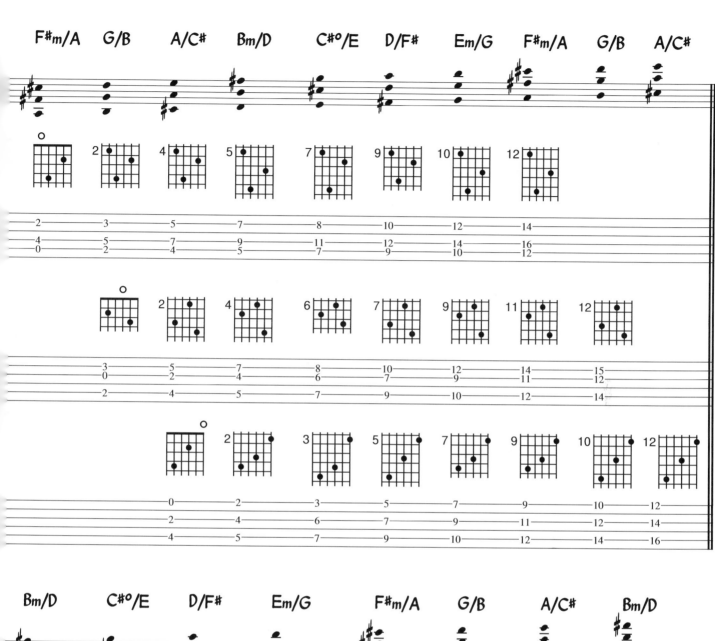
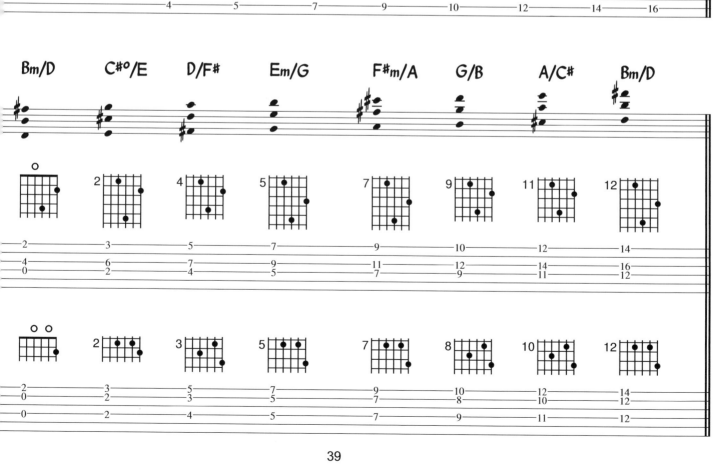

2nd inv. (open voiced)

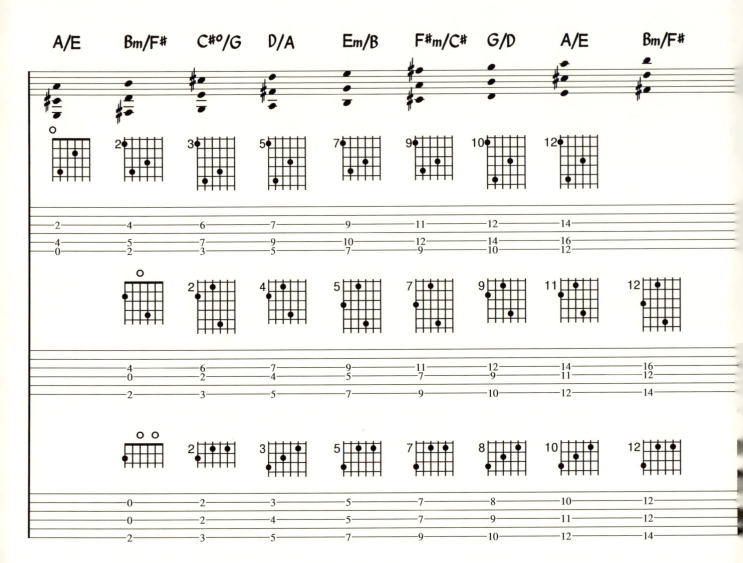

Root Position (open voiced, Version 2)

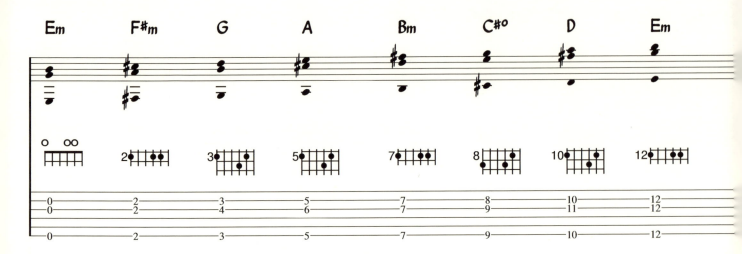

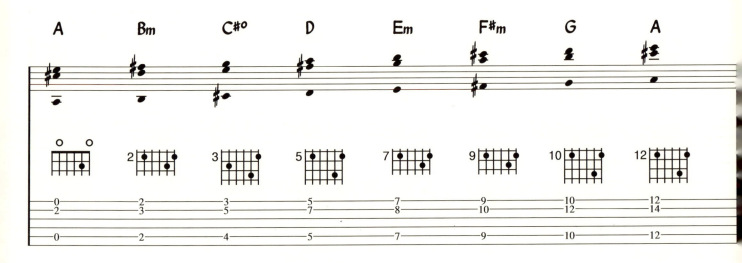

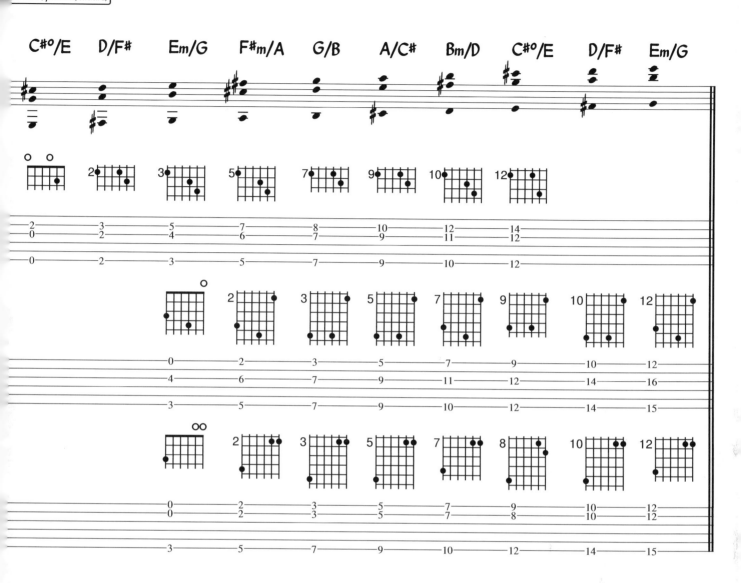
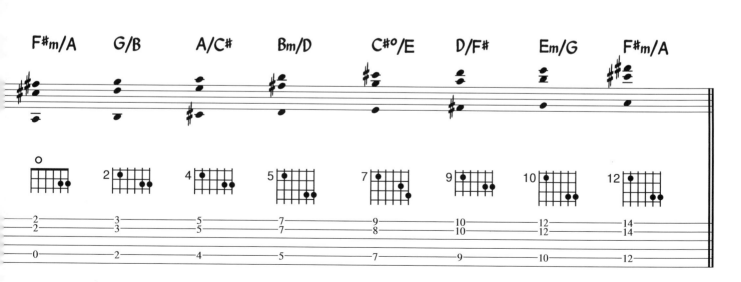

2nd inv. (open voiced, Version 2)

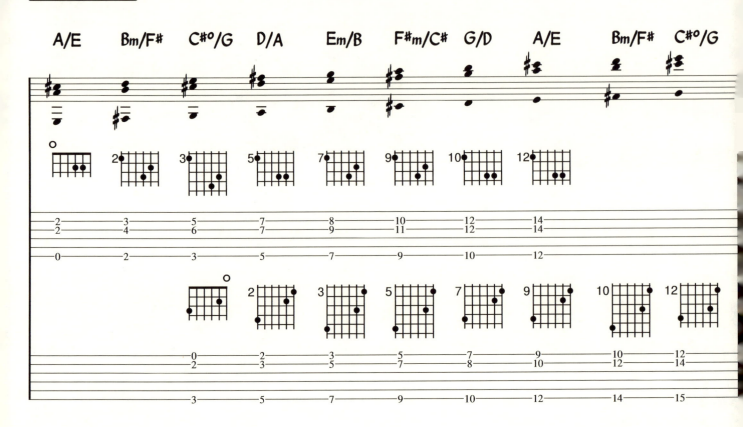
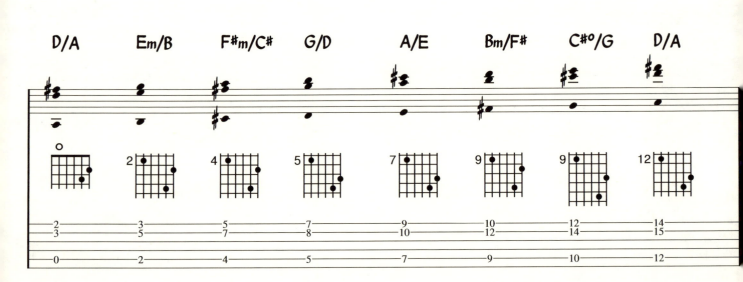

Root Position (open voiced, Version 3)

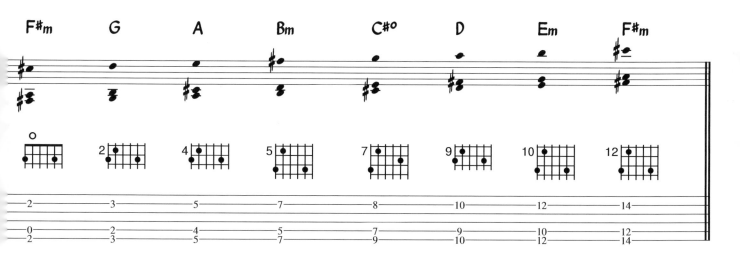

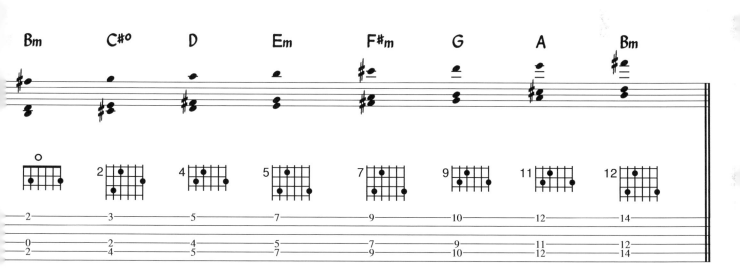

1st inv. (open voiced, Version 3)

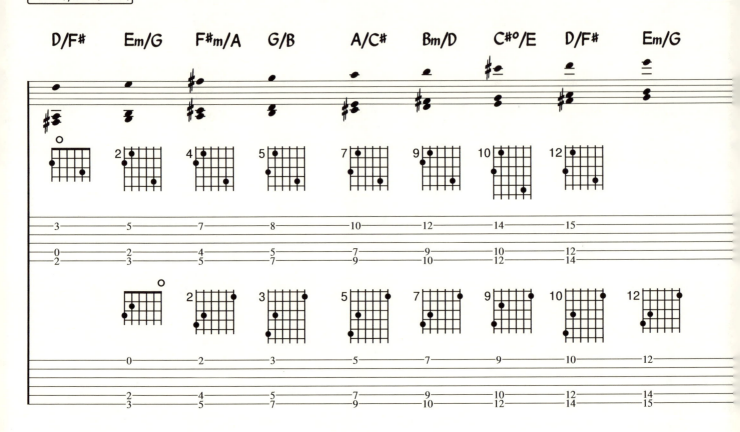
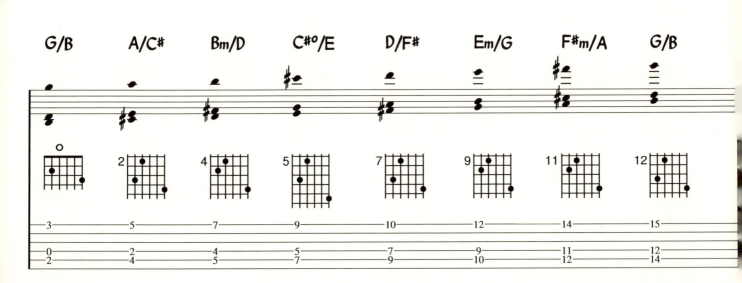

2nd inv. (open voiced, Version 3)

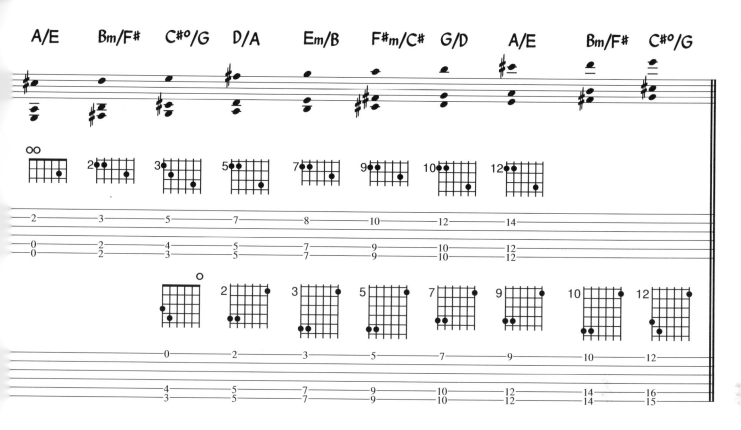
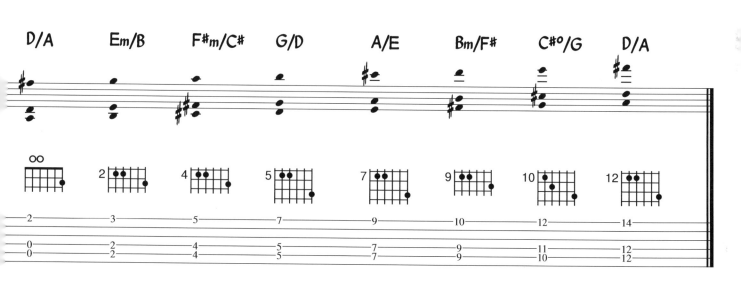

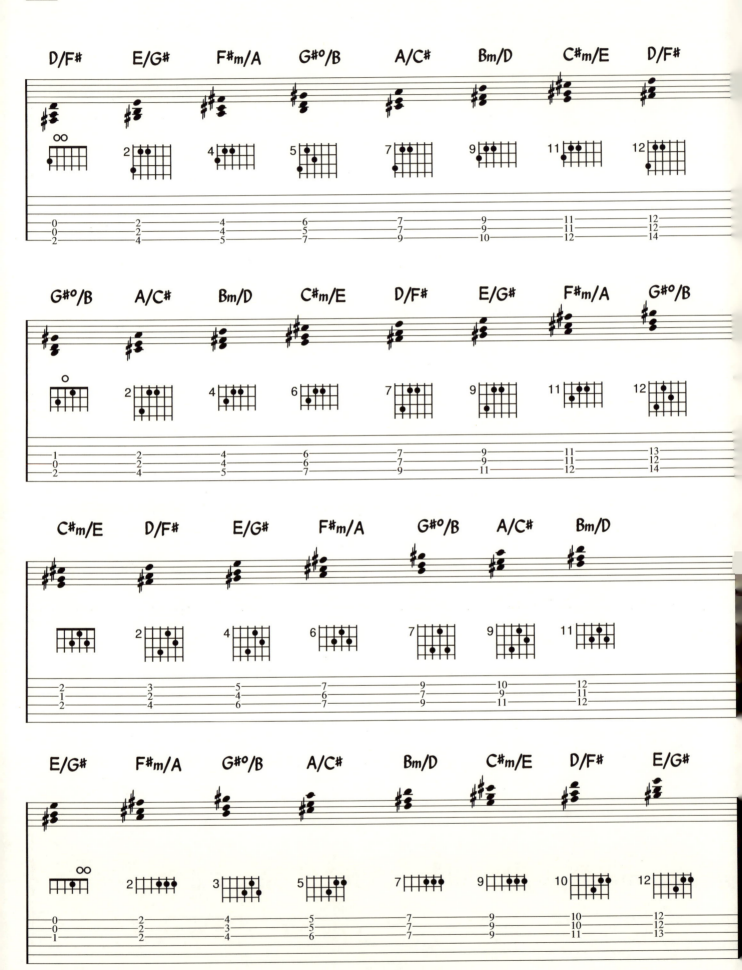

Root Position (open voiced)

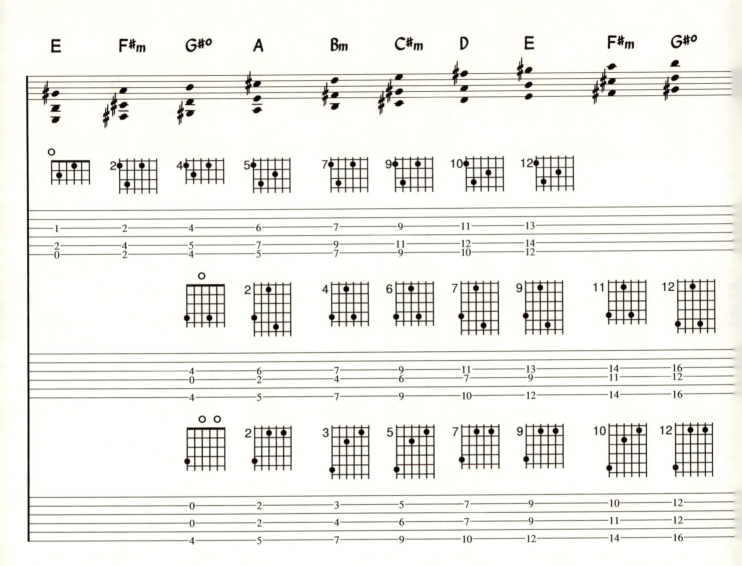

1st inv. (open voiced)

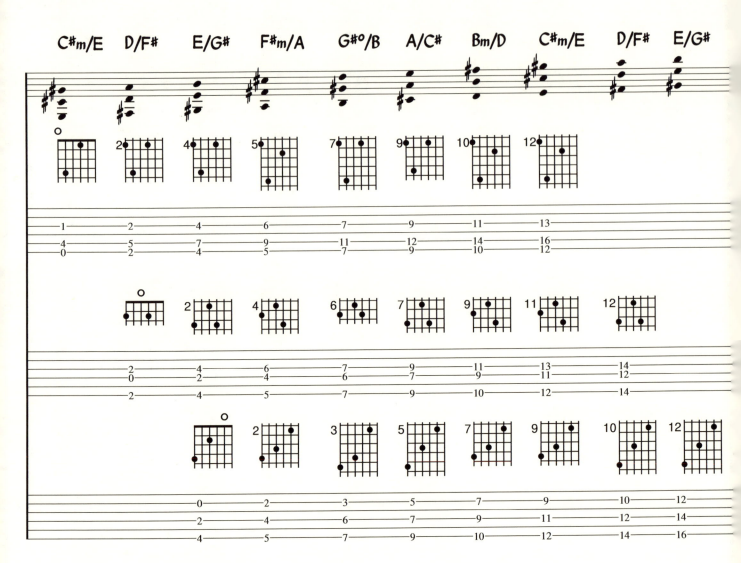

54

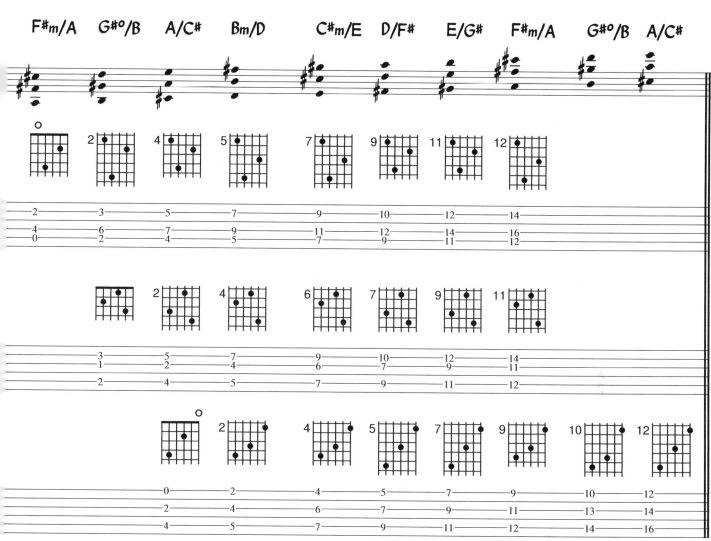
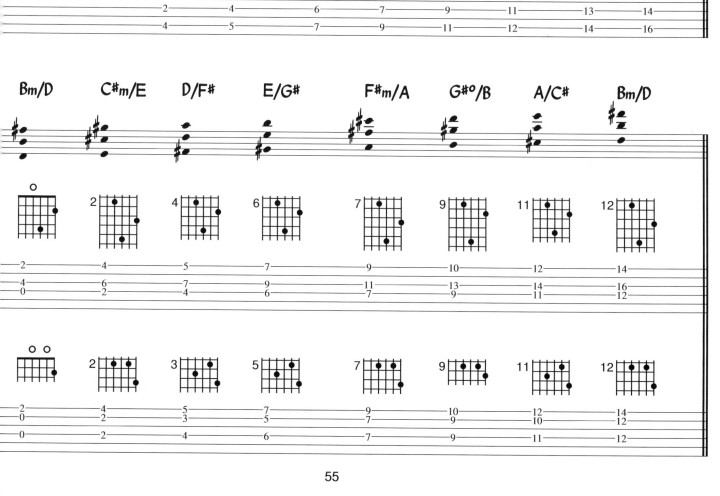

2nd inv. (open voiced)

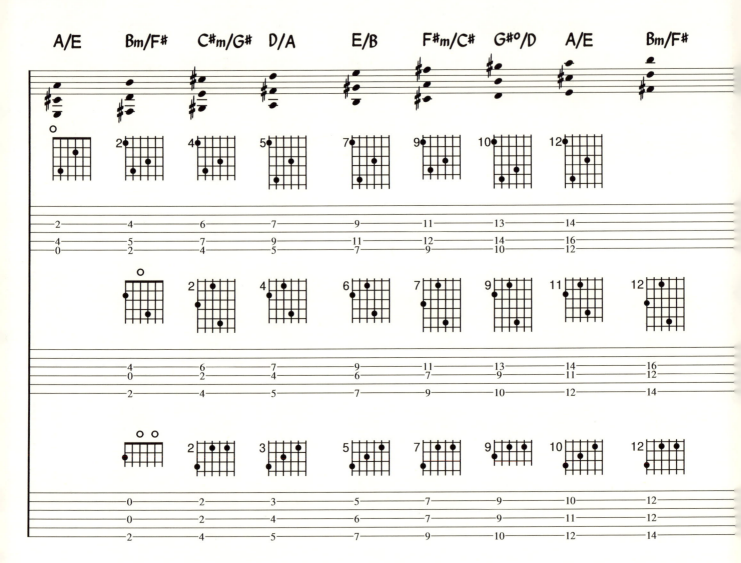

56

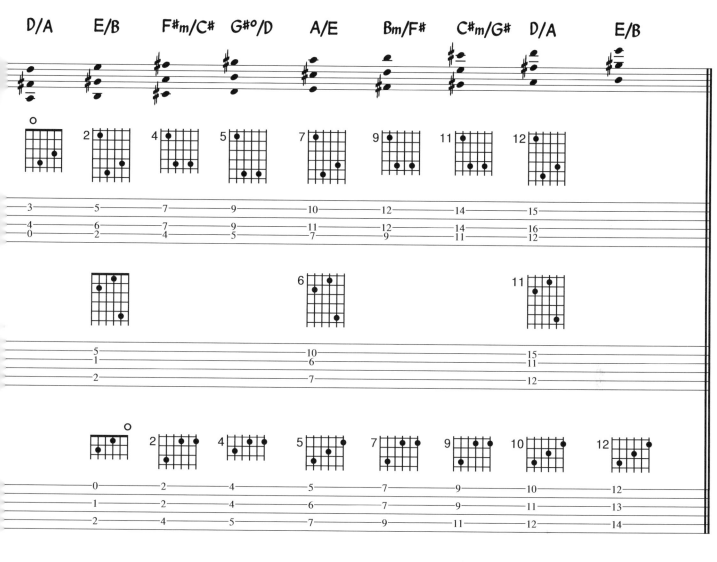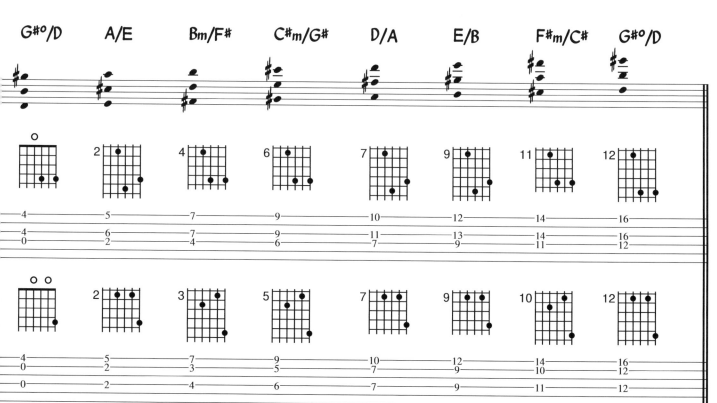

Root Position (open voiced, Version 2)

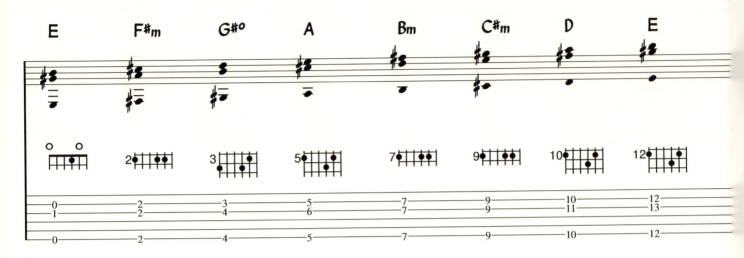
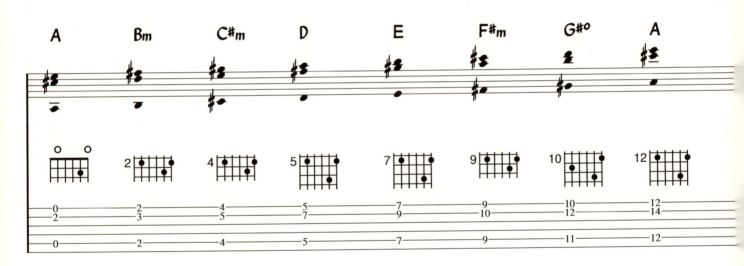

58

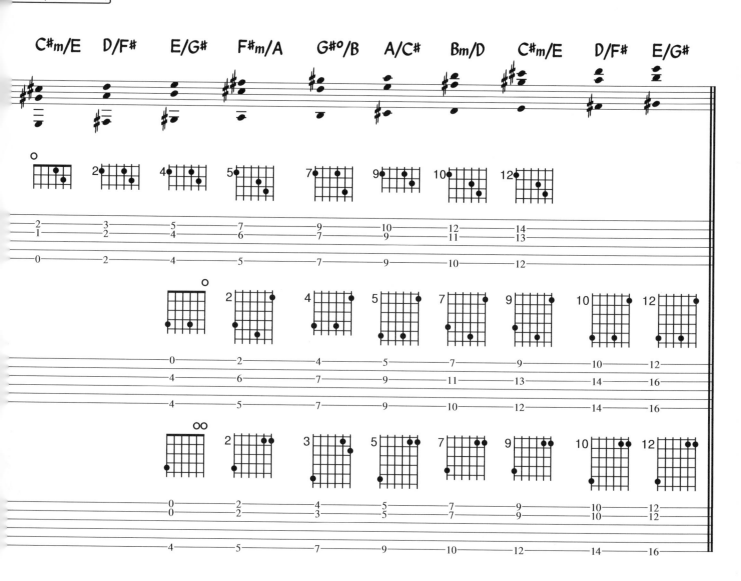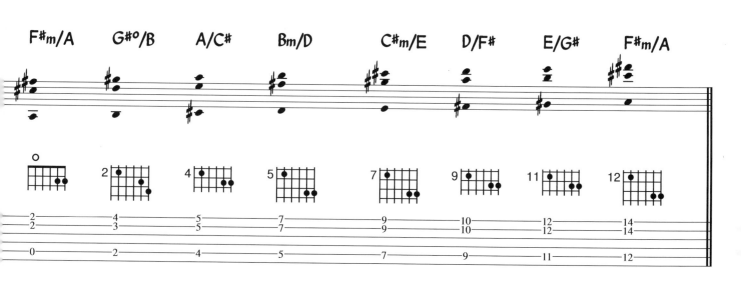

2nd inv. (open voiced, Version 2)

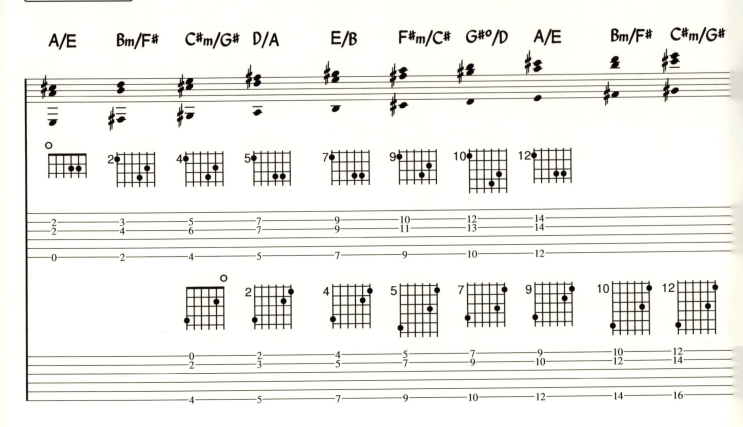
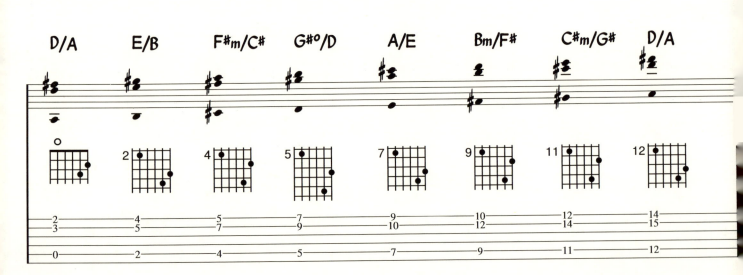

Root Position (open voiced, Version 3)

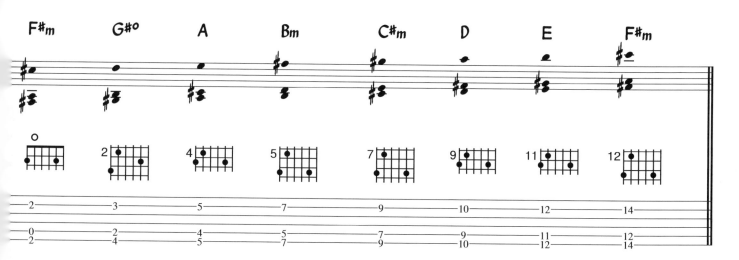

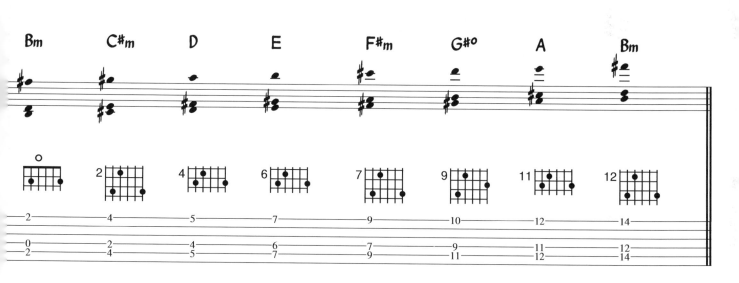

1st inv. (open voiced, Version 3)

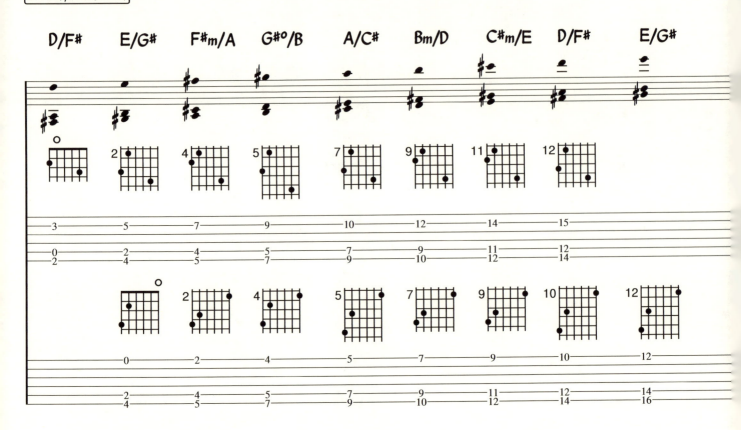
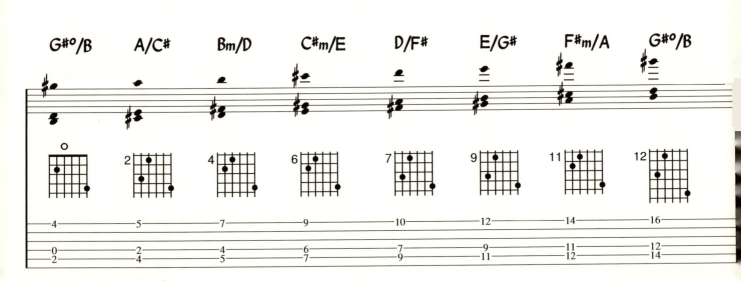

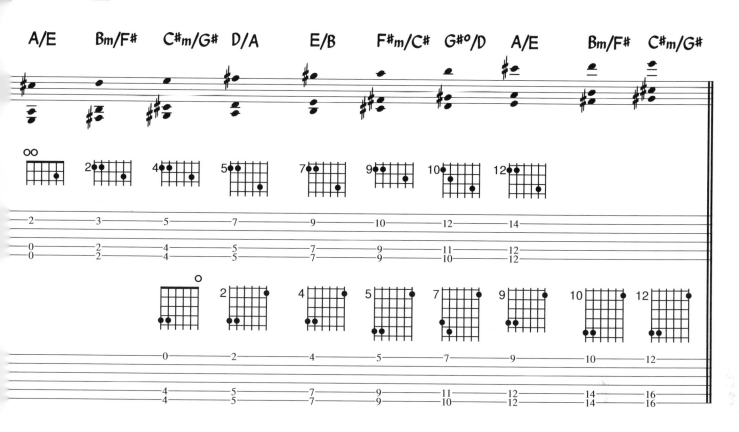
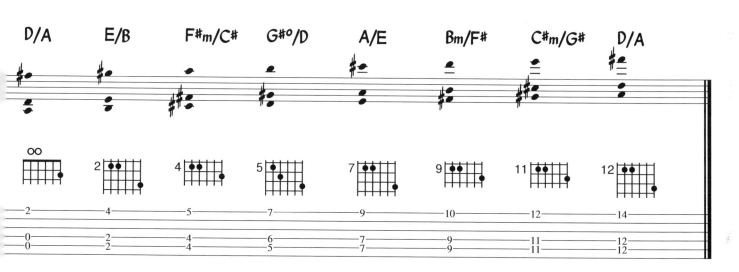

~ E major ~

Root Position (open voiced)

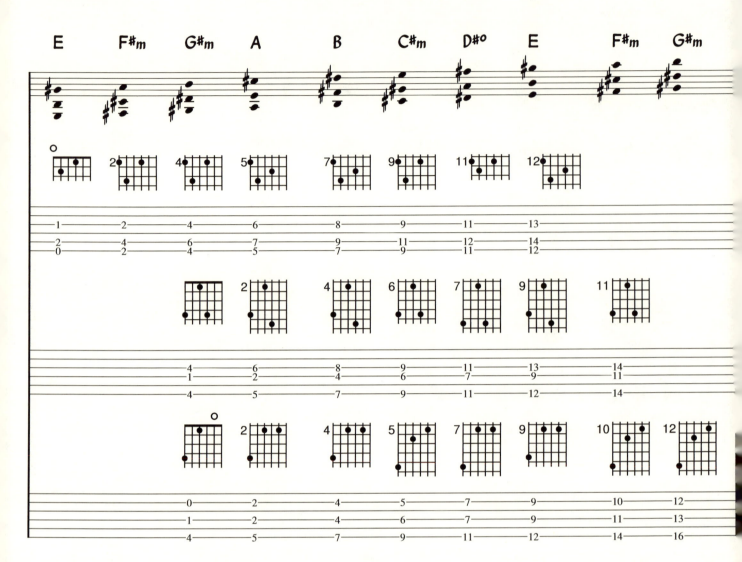

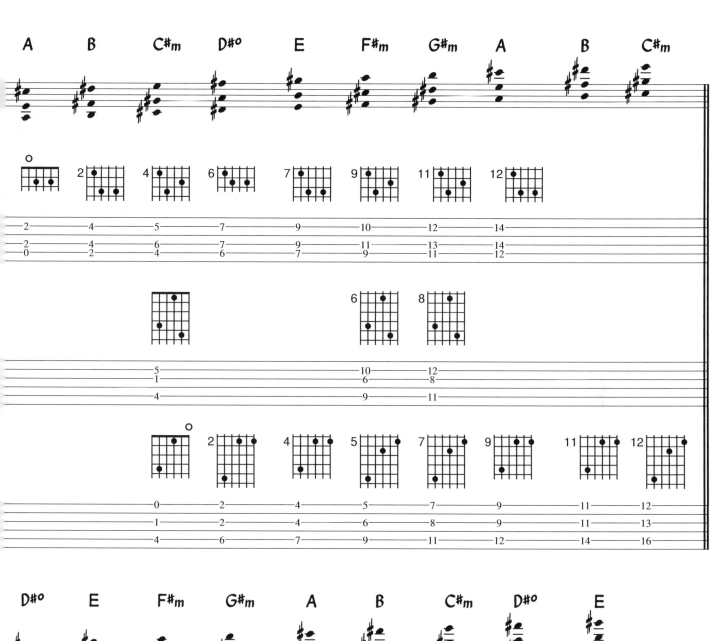
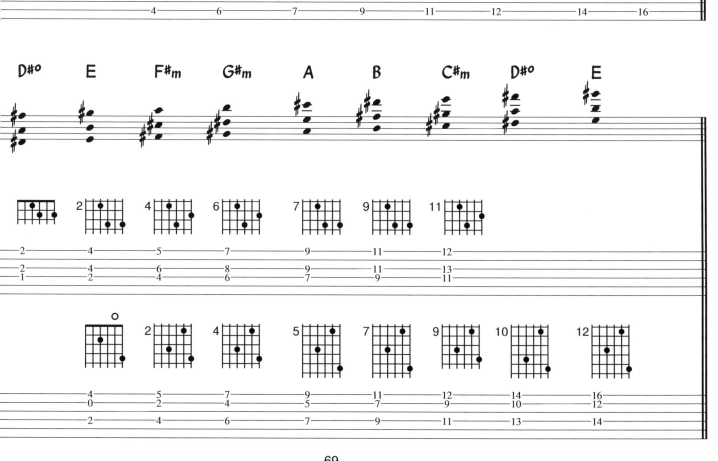

1st inv. (open voiced)

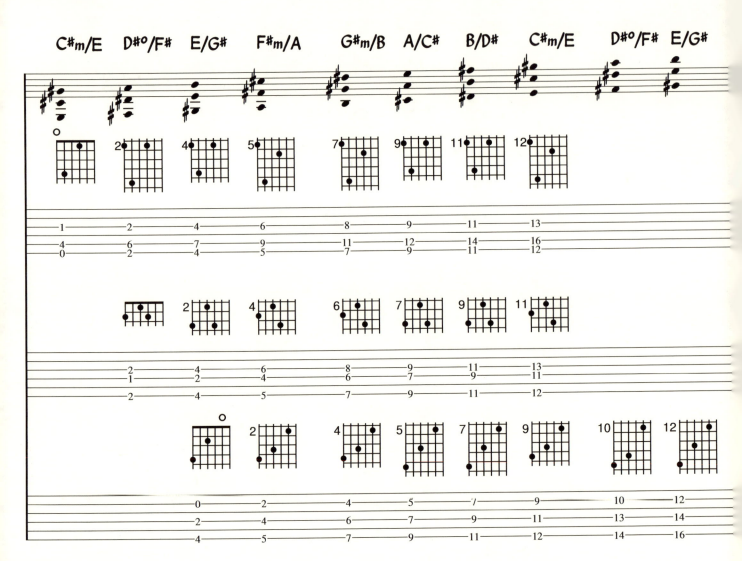

70

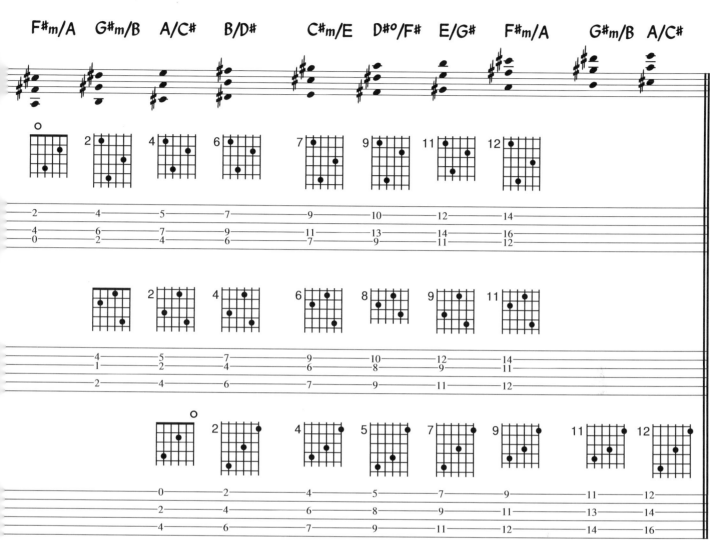
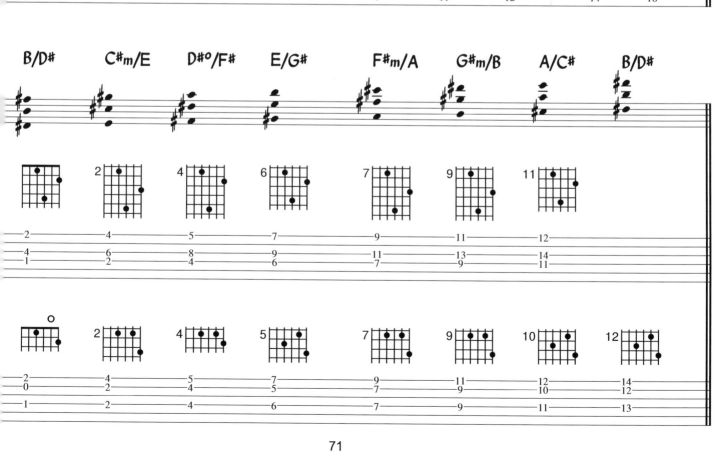

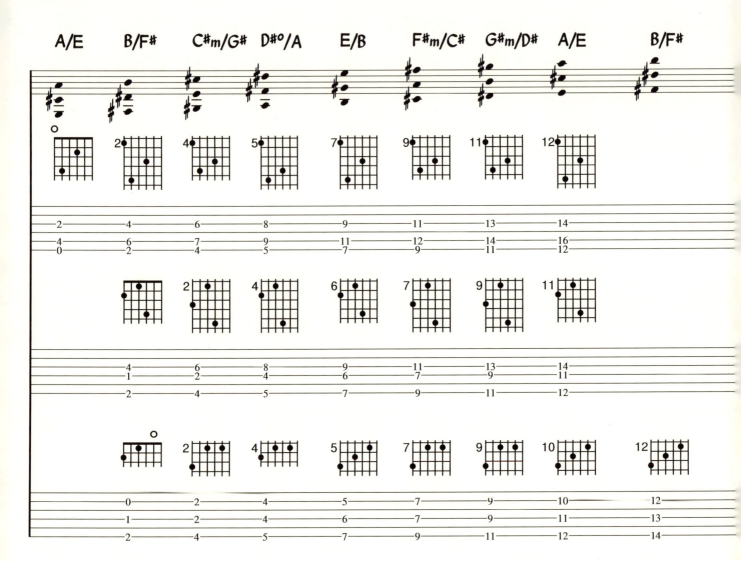

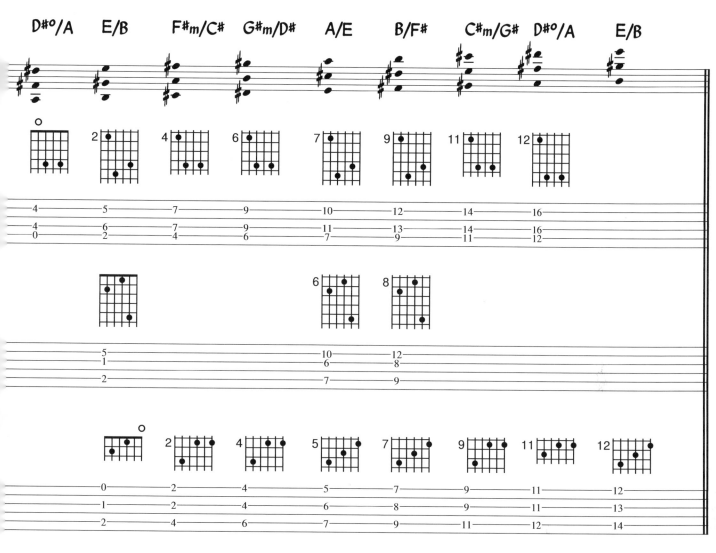
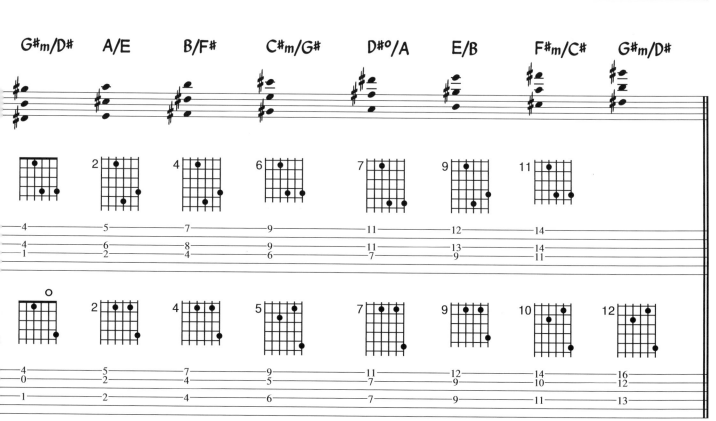

Root Position (open voiced, Version 2)

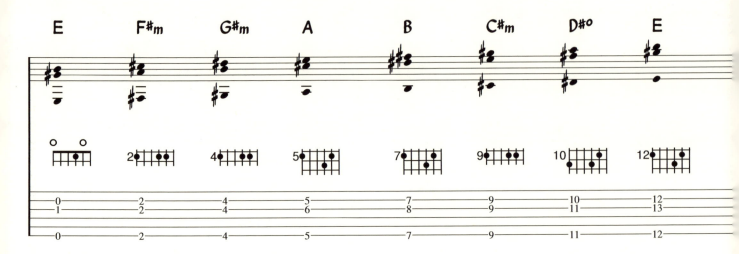

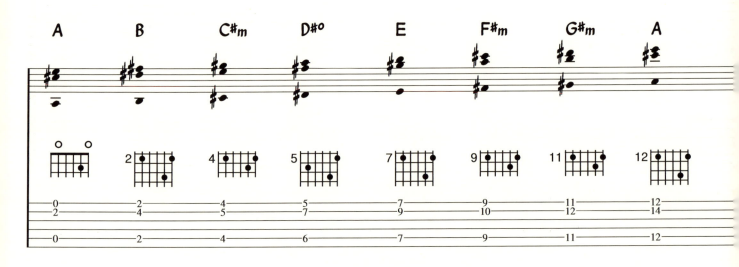

st inv. (open voiced, Version 2)

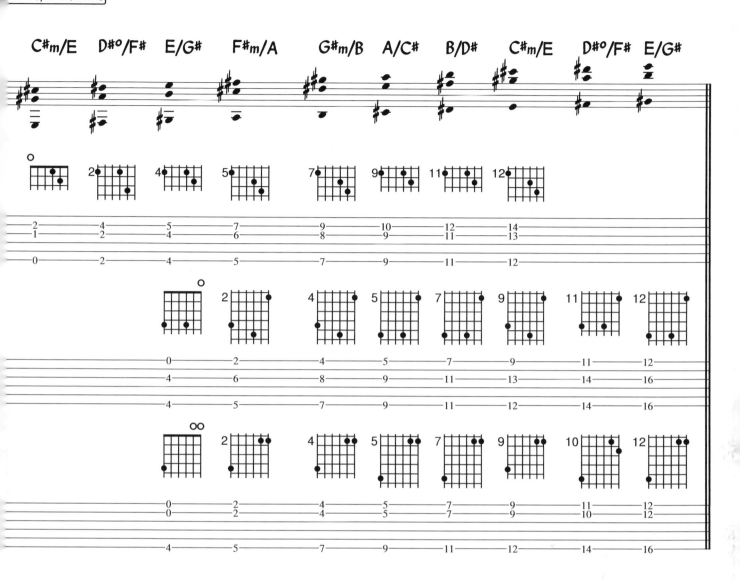

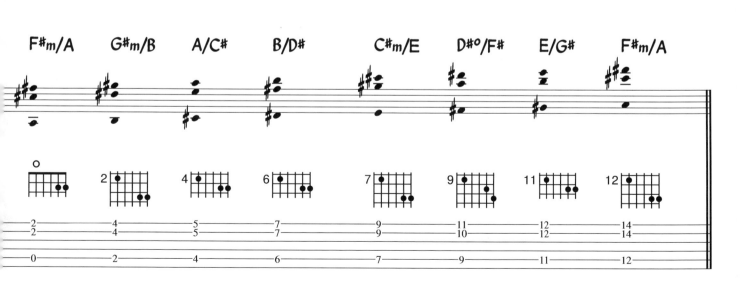

2nd inv. (open voiced, Version 2)

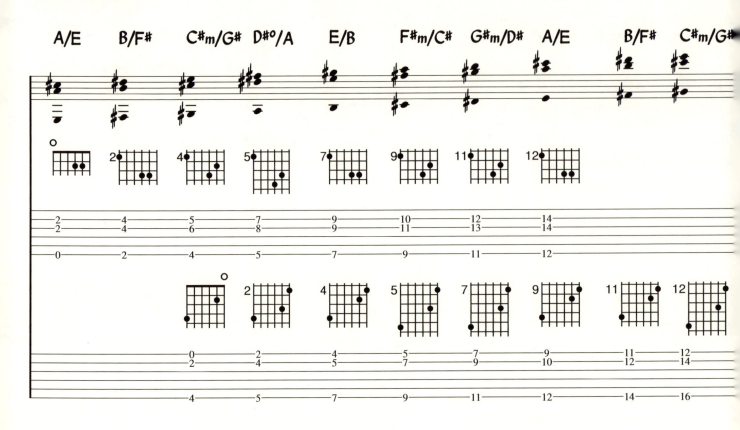
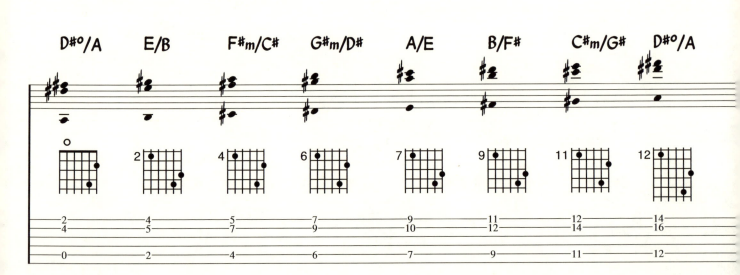

Root Position (open voiced, Version 3)

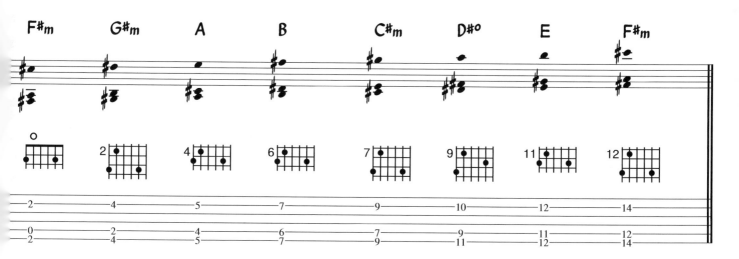

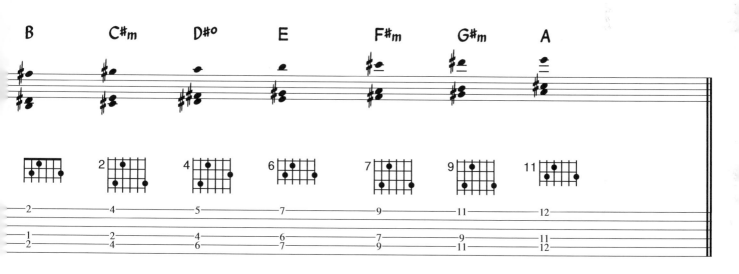

1st inv. (open voiced, Version 3)

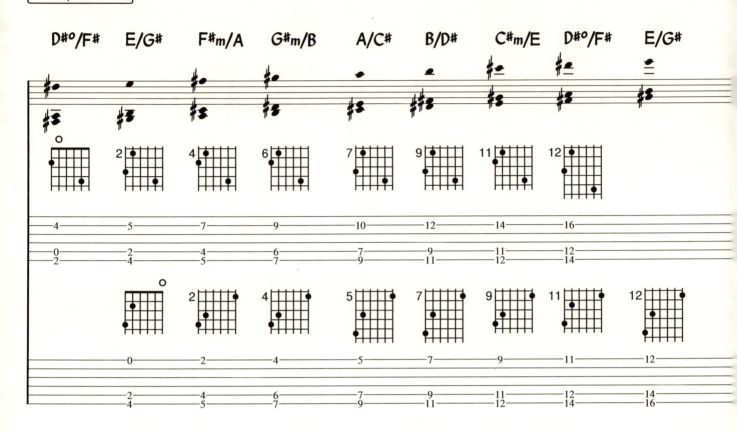
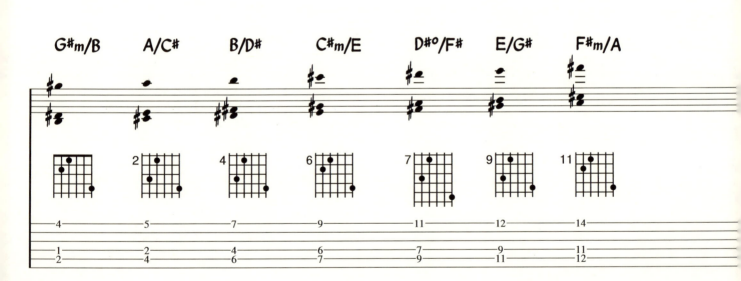

78

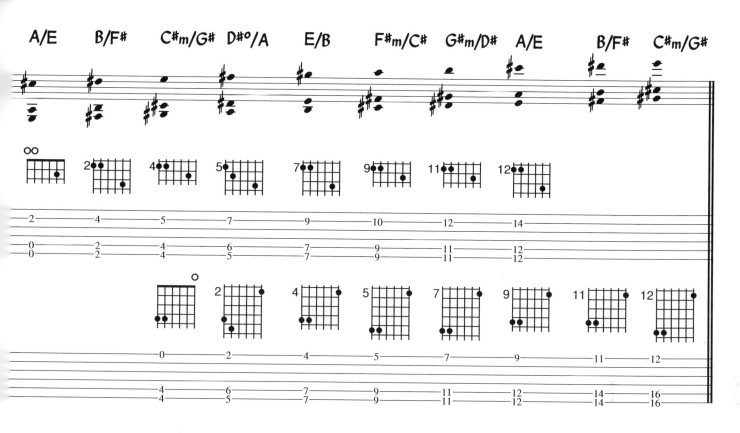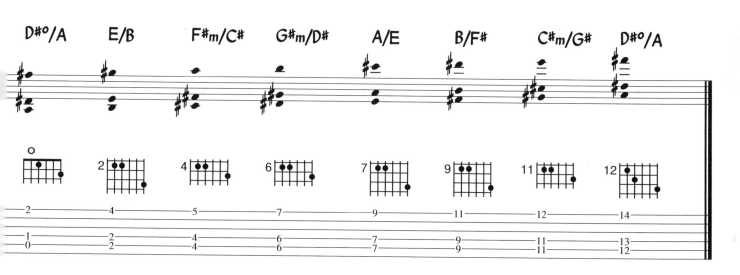

~ B major ~

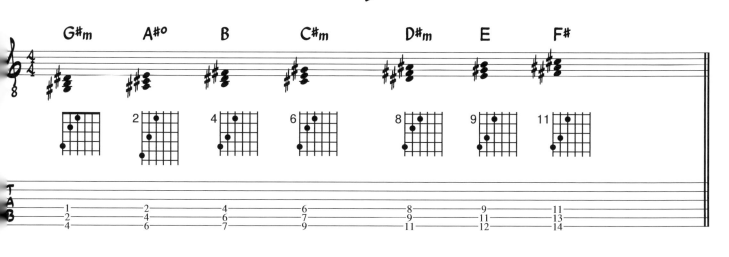
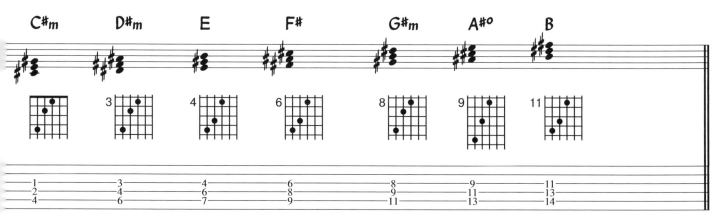
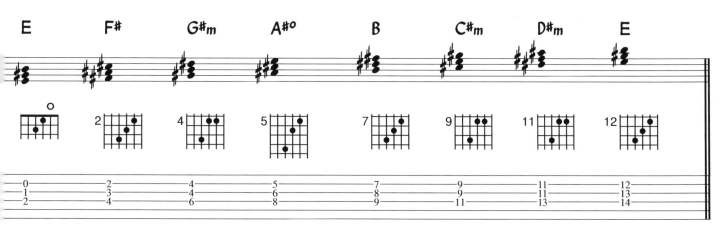
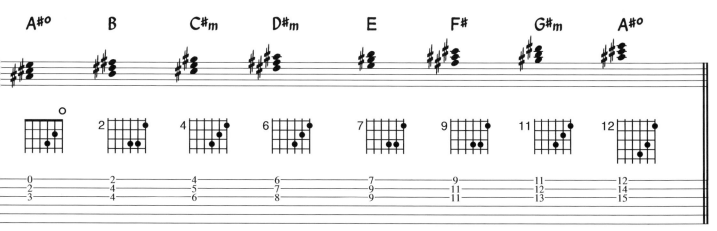

Root Position (open voiced)

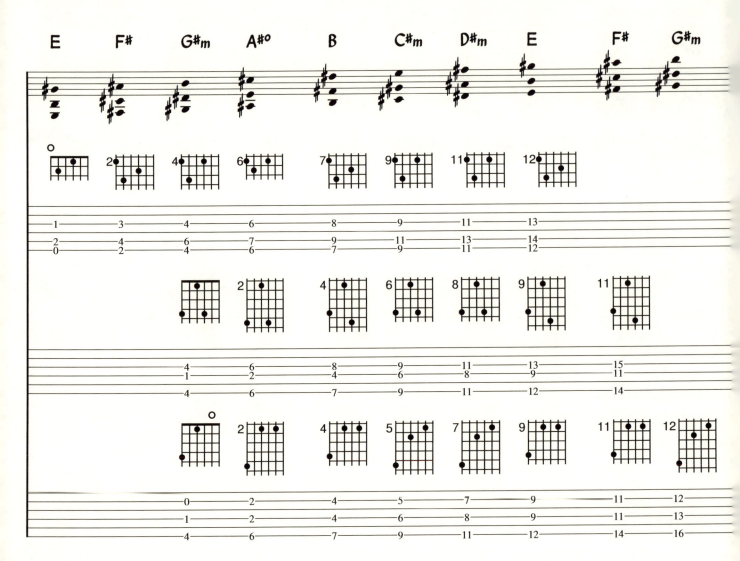

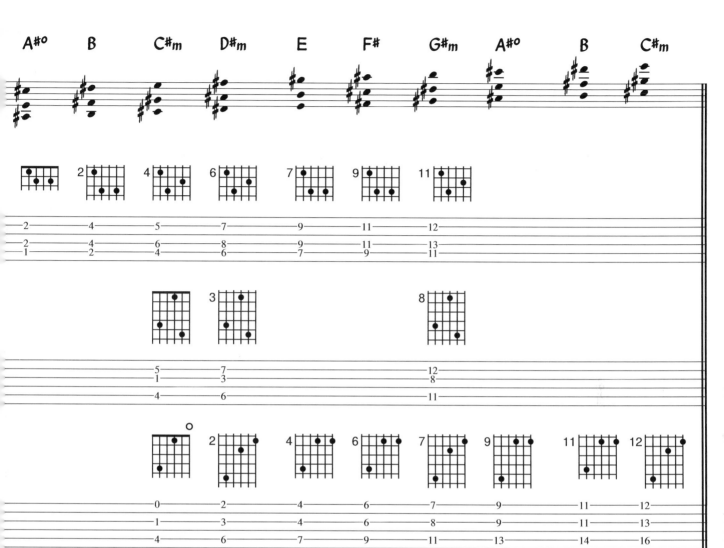
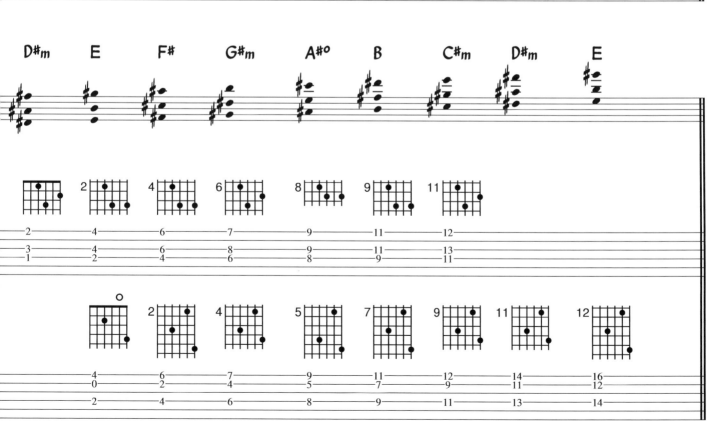

1st inv. (open voiced)

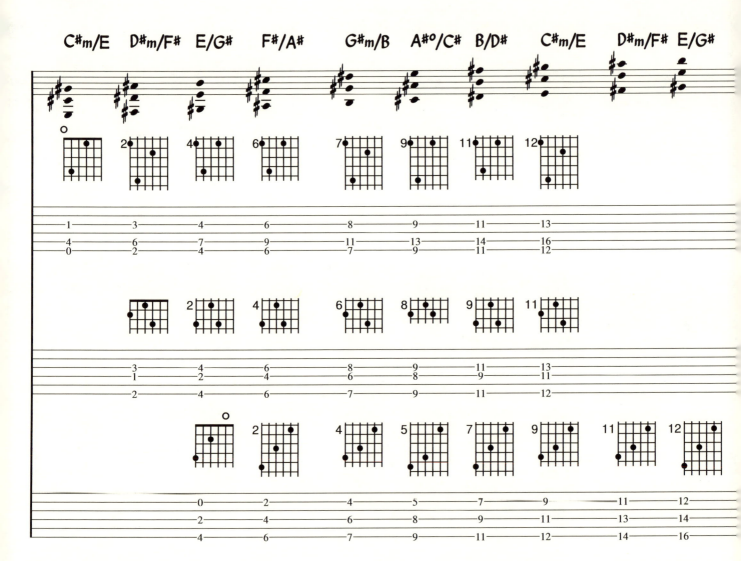

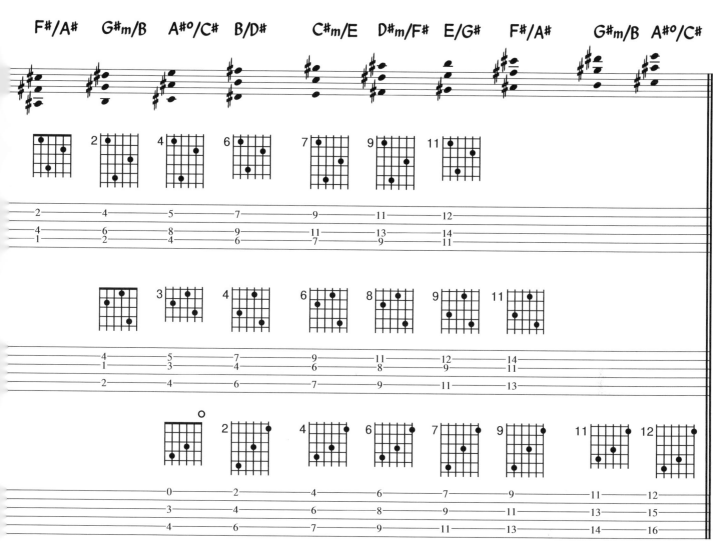
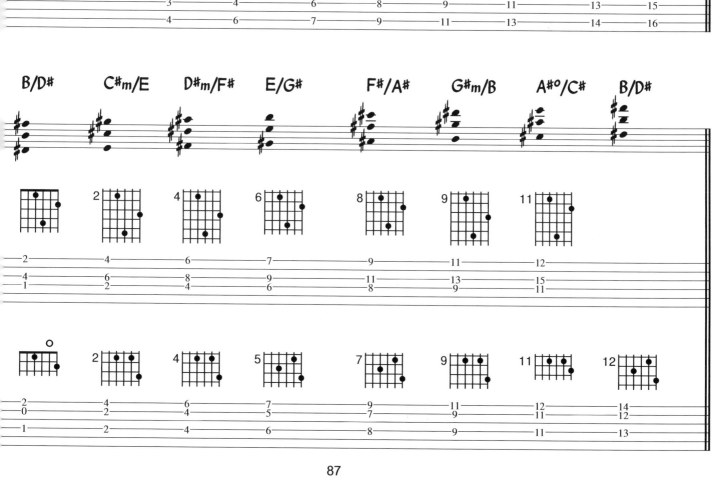

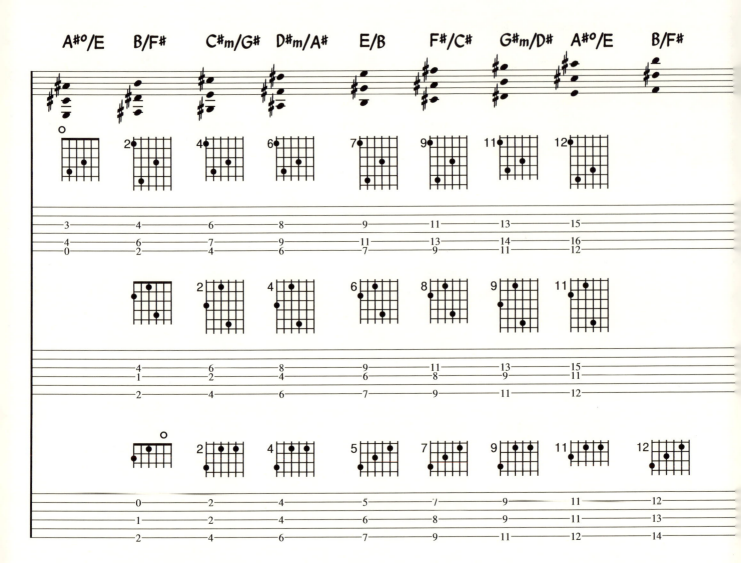

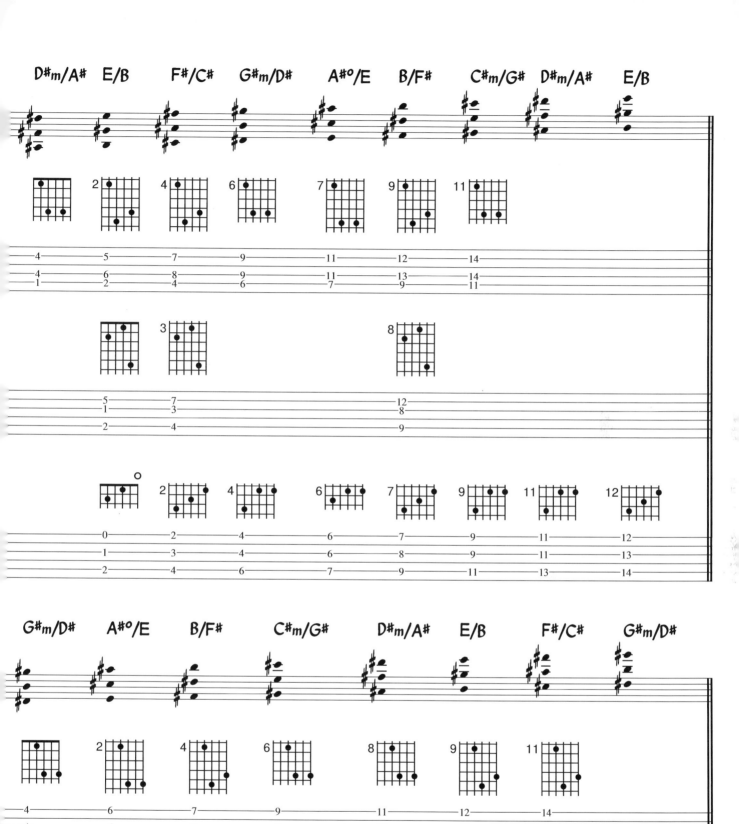

Root Position (open voiced, Version 2)

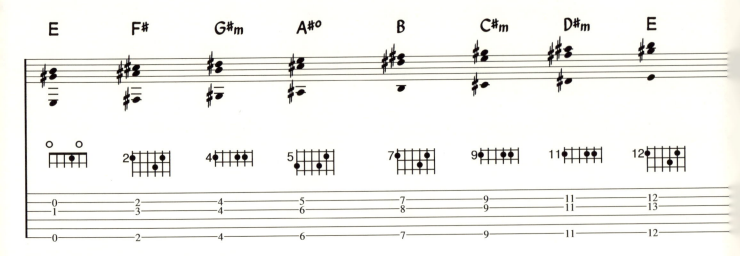
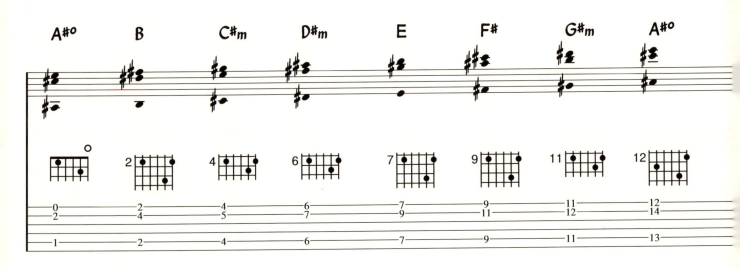

90

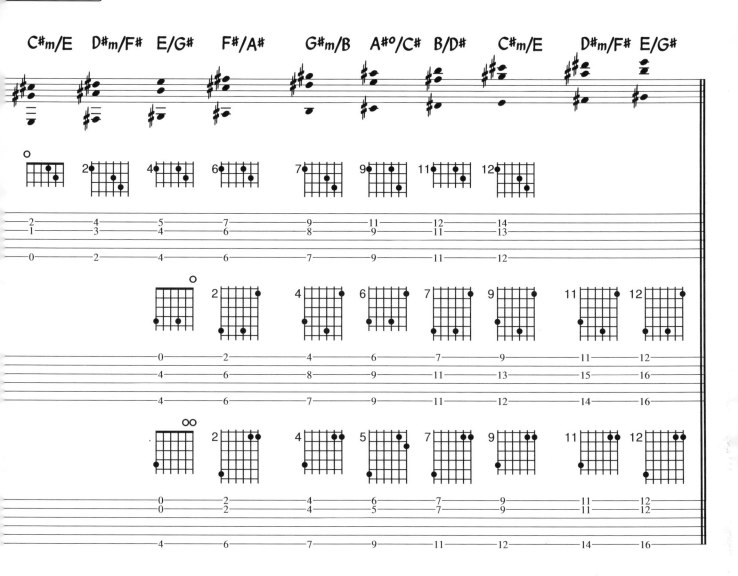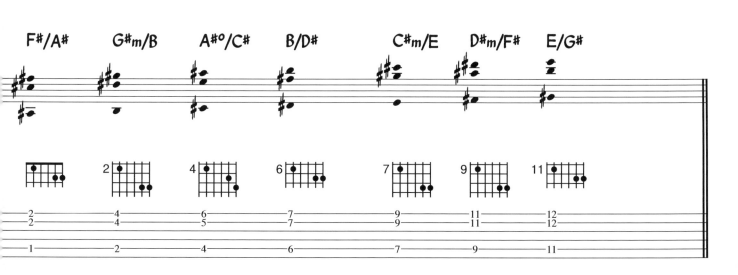

2nd inv. (open voiced, Version 2)

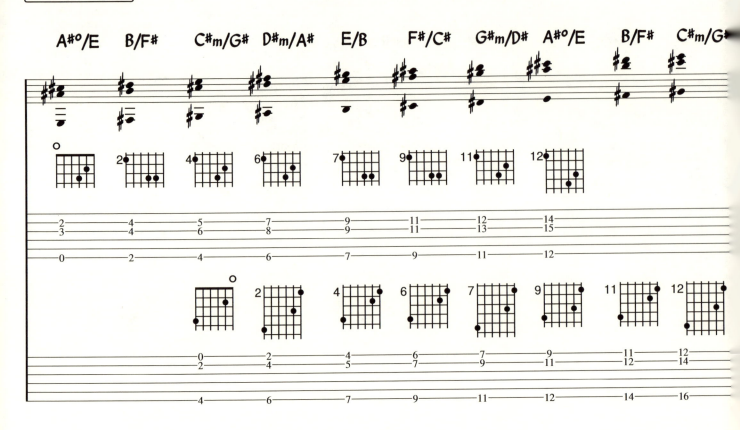
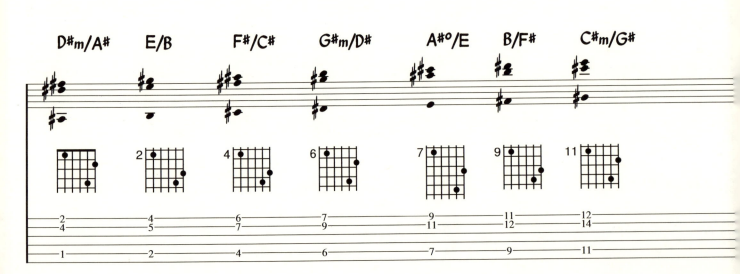

92

Root Position (open voiced, Version 3)

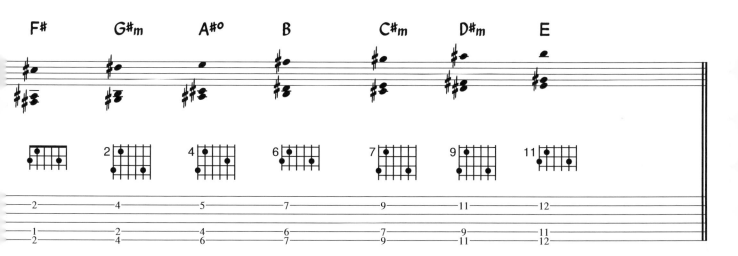

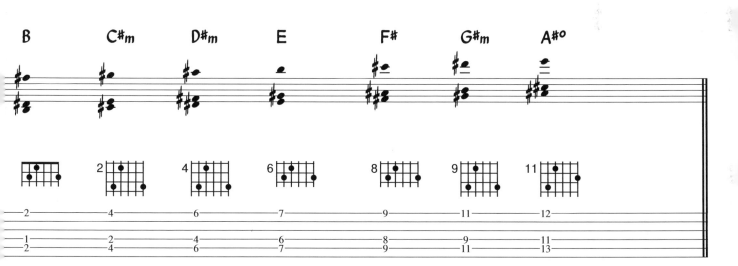

1st inv. (open voiced, Version 3)

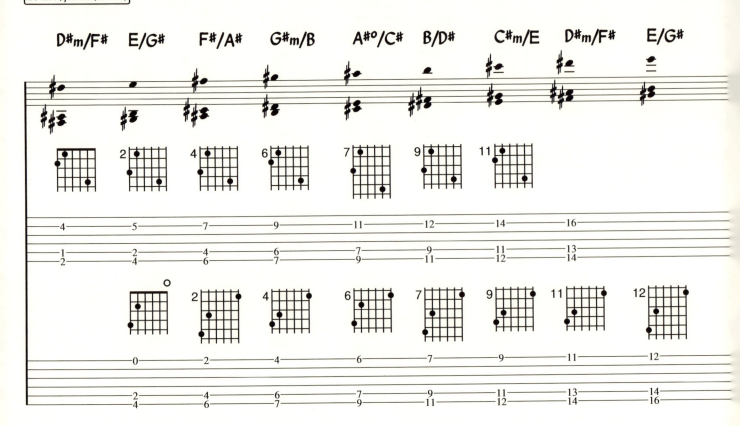
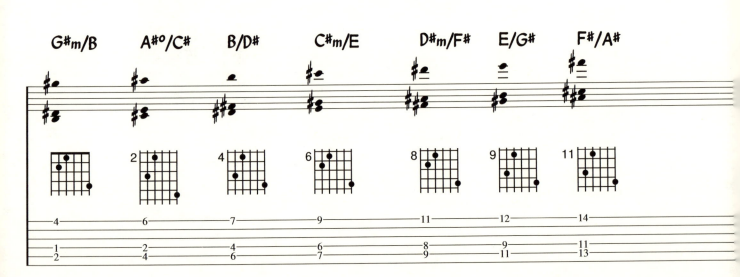

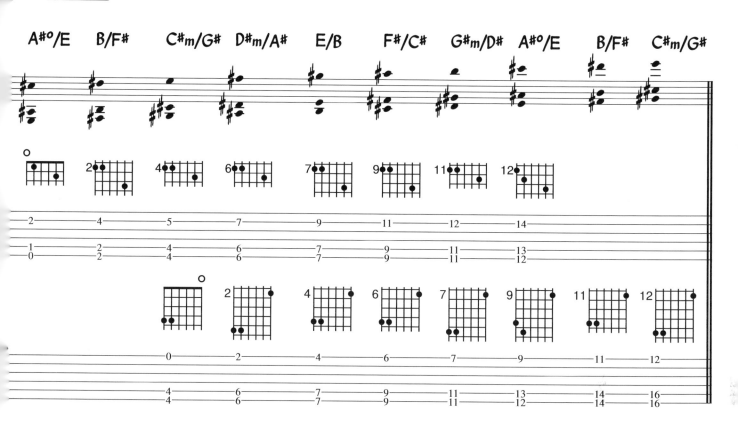
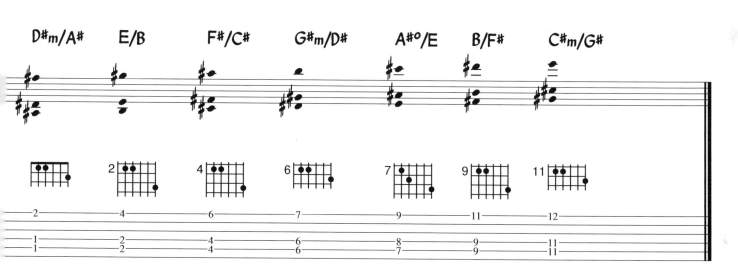

Gb major

Root Position (open voiced)

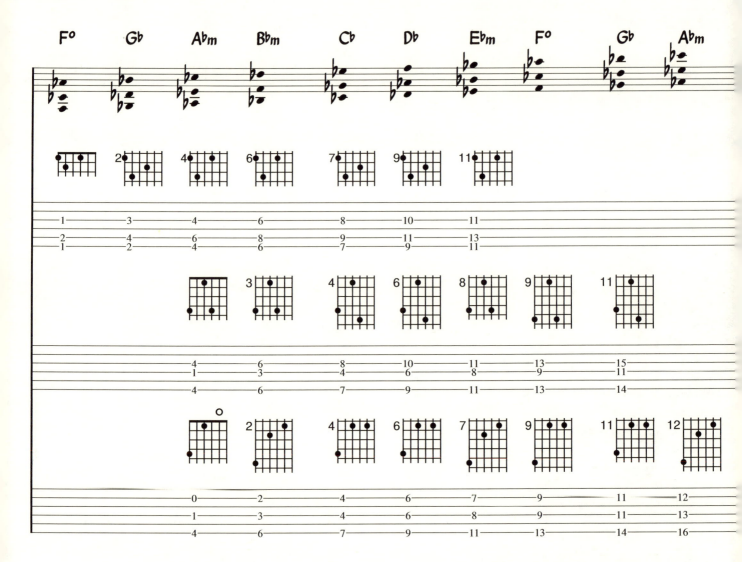

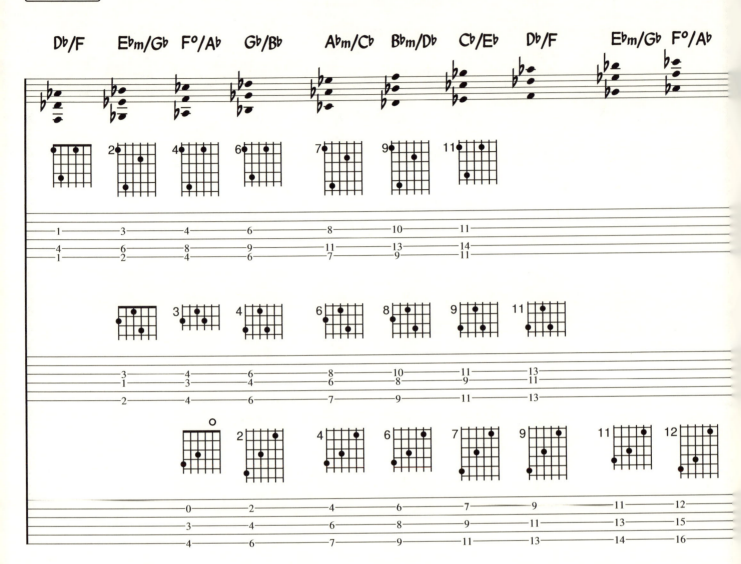

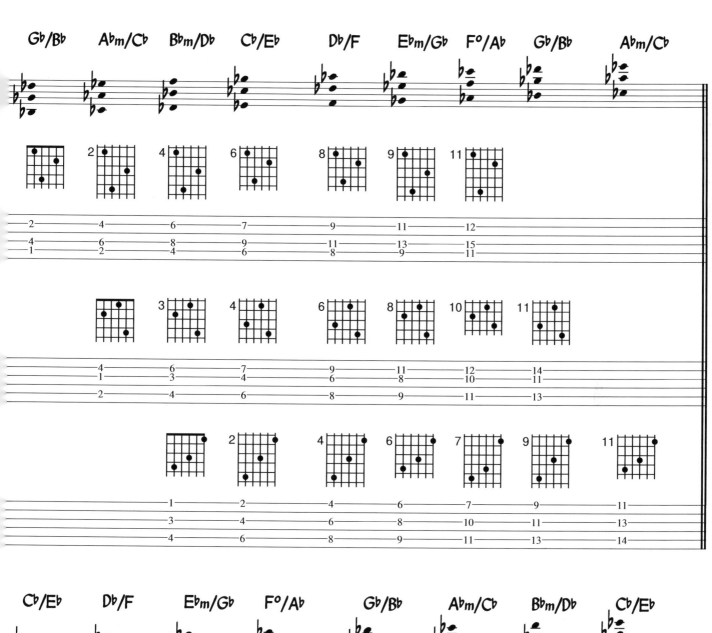
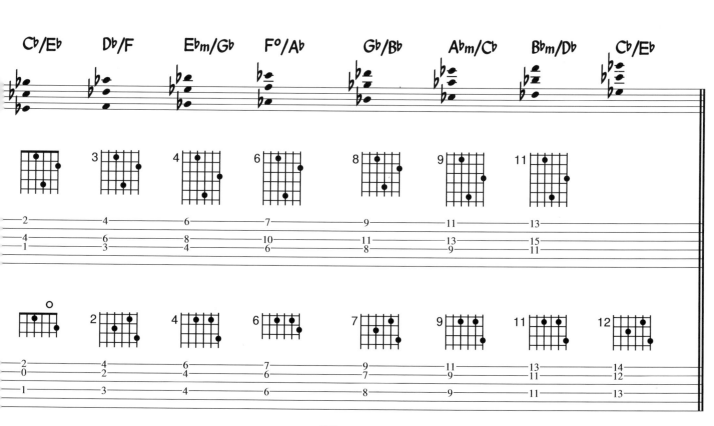

2nd inv. (open voiced)

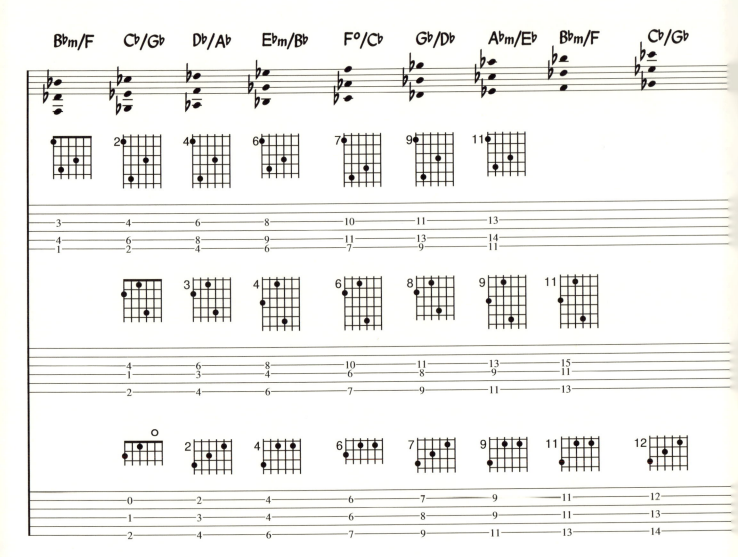

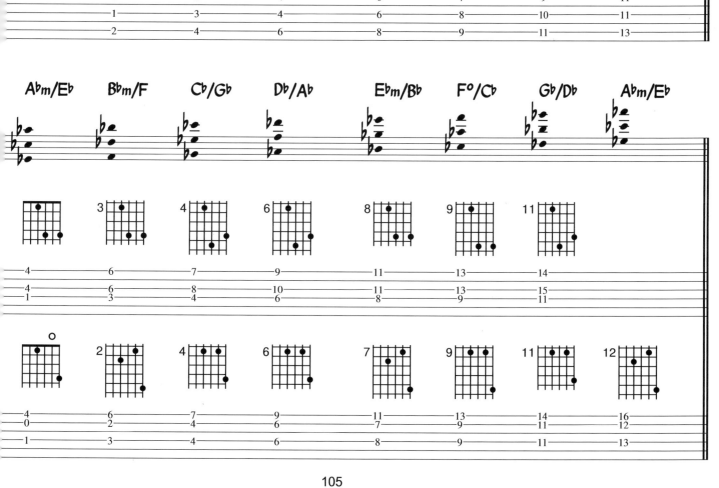

Root Position (open voiced, Version 2)

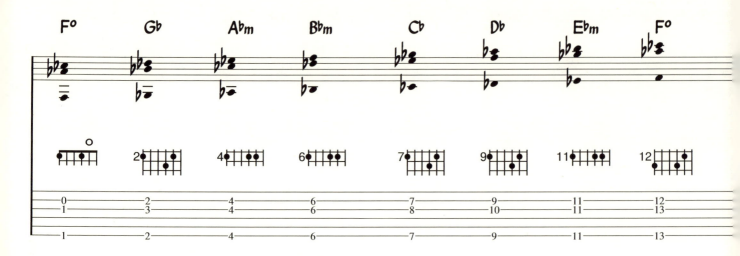
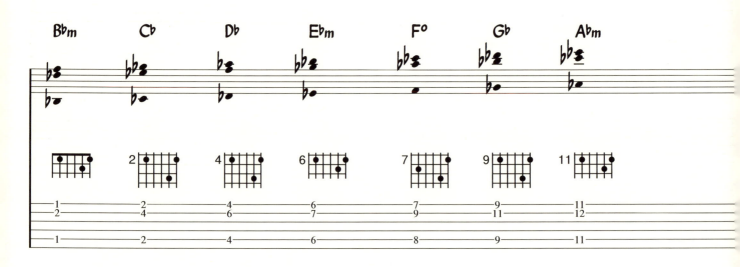

t inv. (open voiced, Version 2)

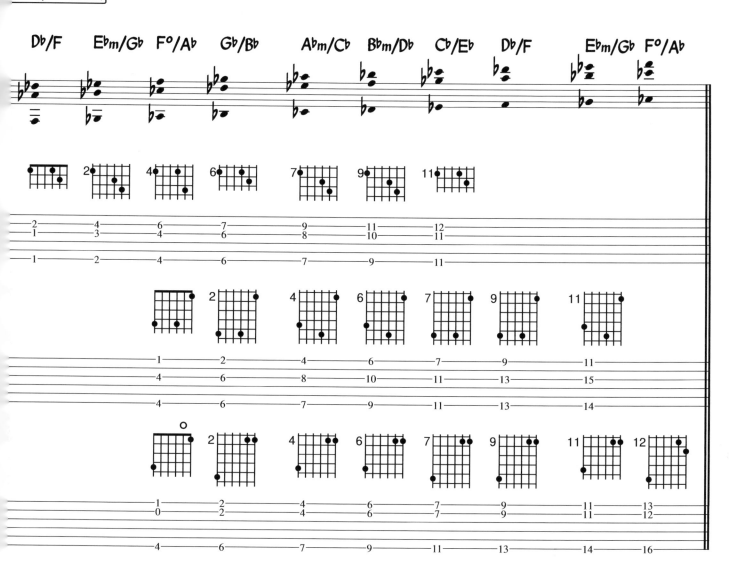

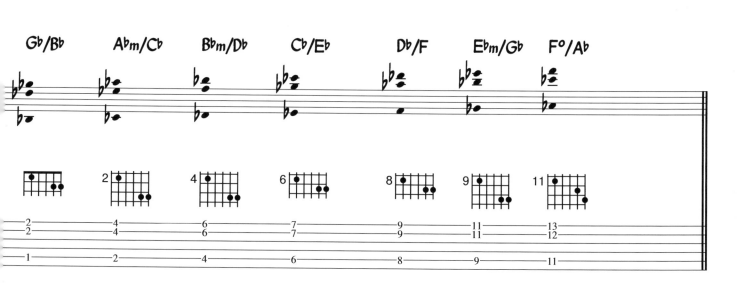

2nd inv. (open voiced, Version 2)

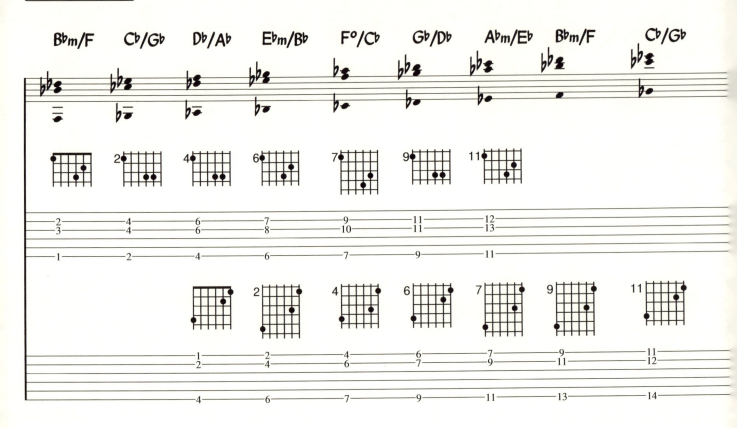
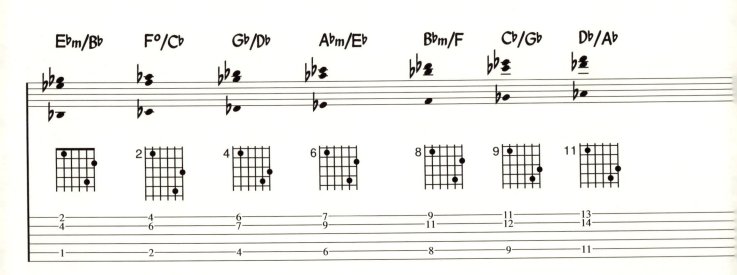

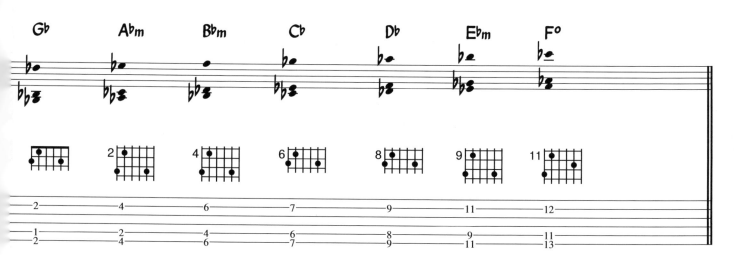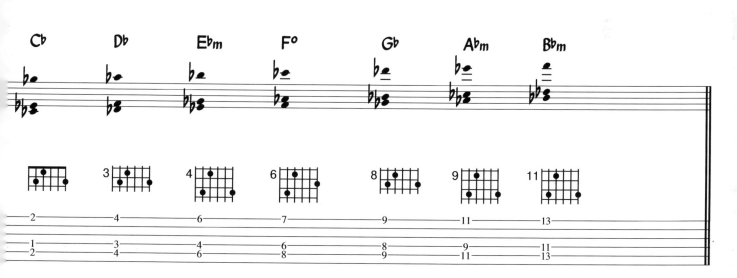

1st inv. (open voiced, Version 3)

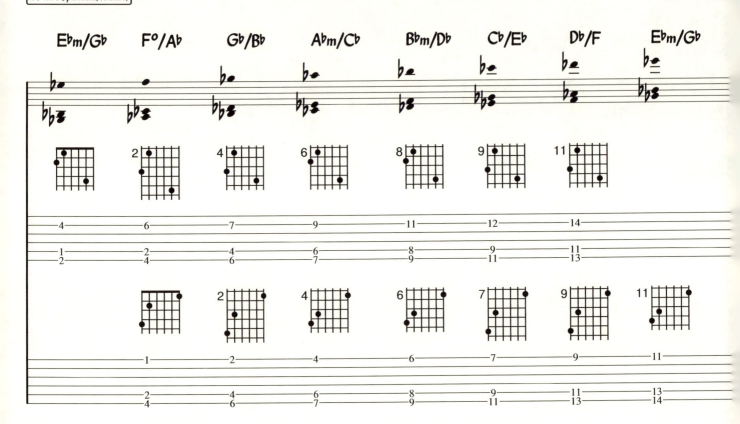
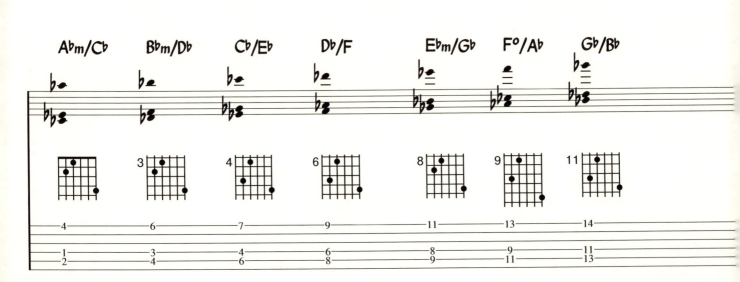

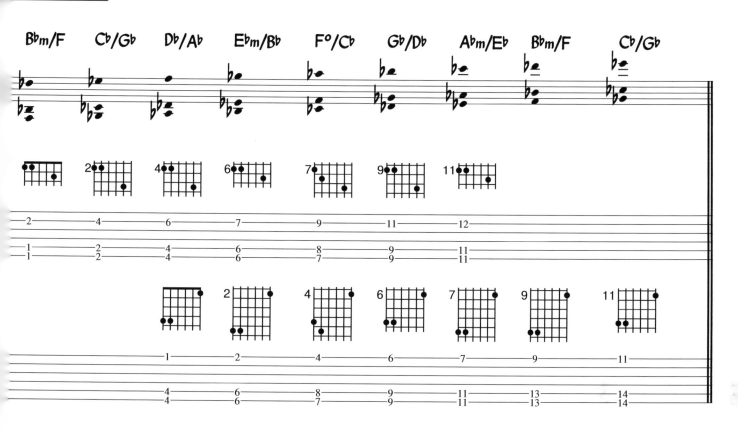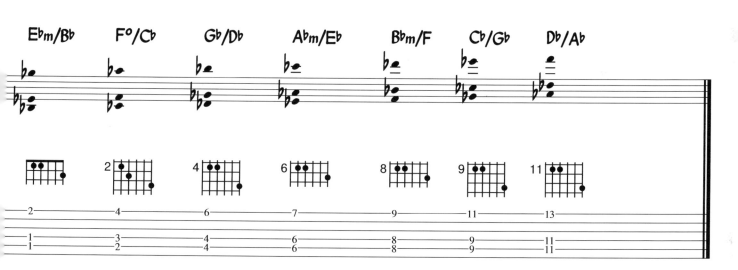

Root Position (open voiced)

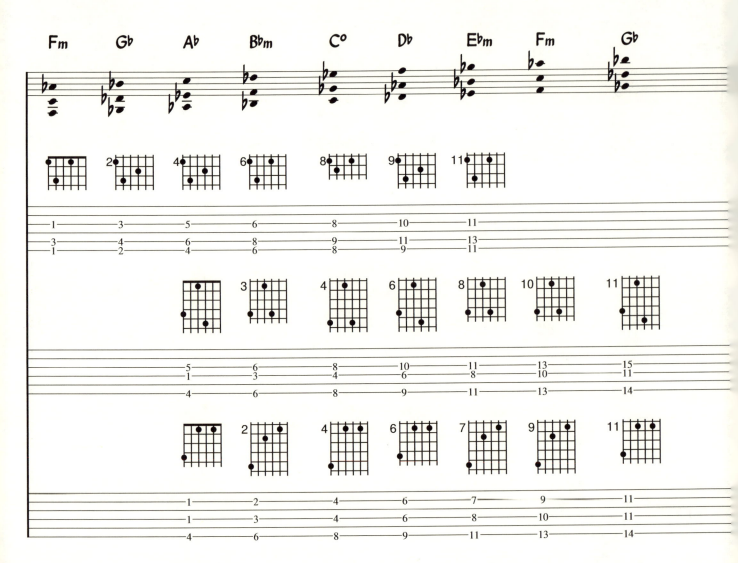

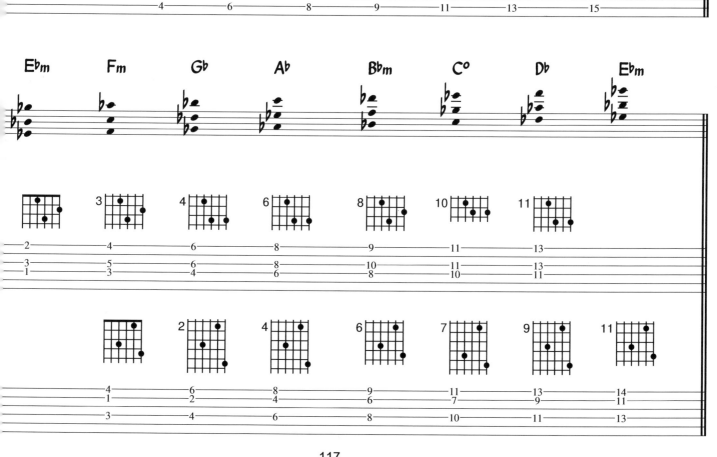

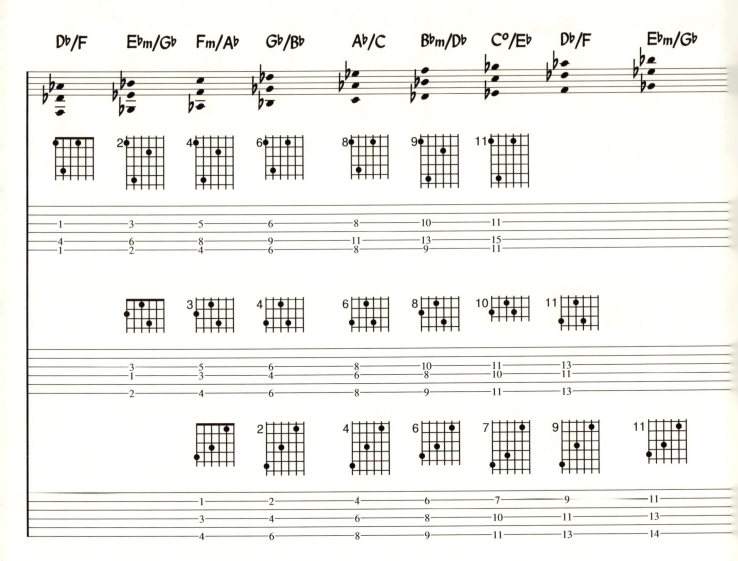

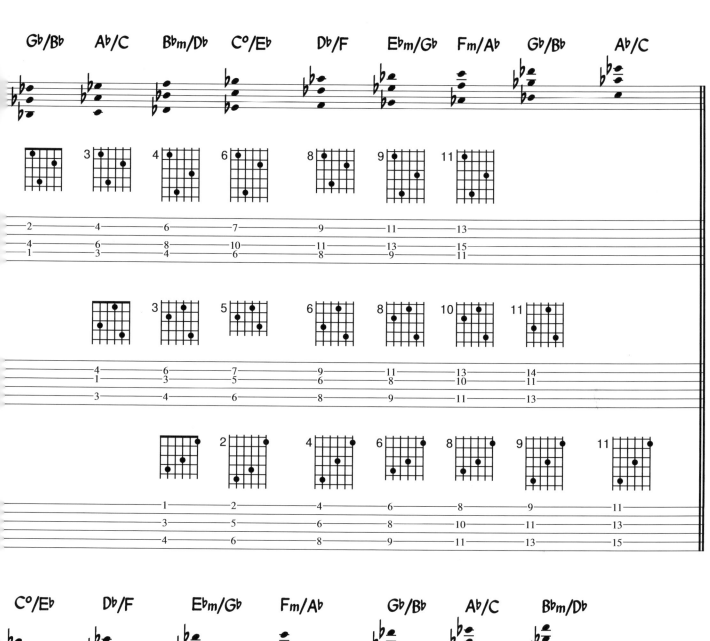
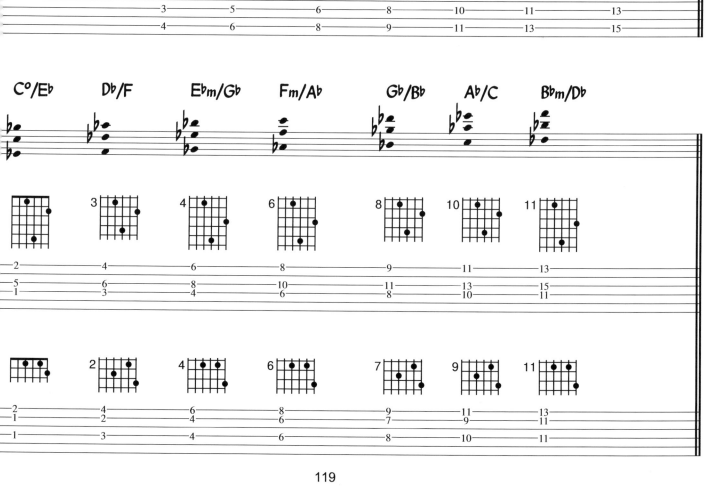

2nd inv. (open voiced)

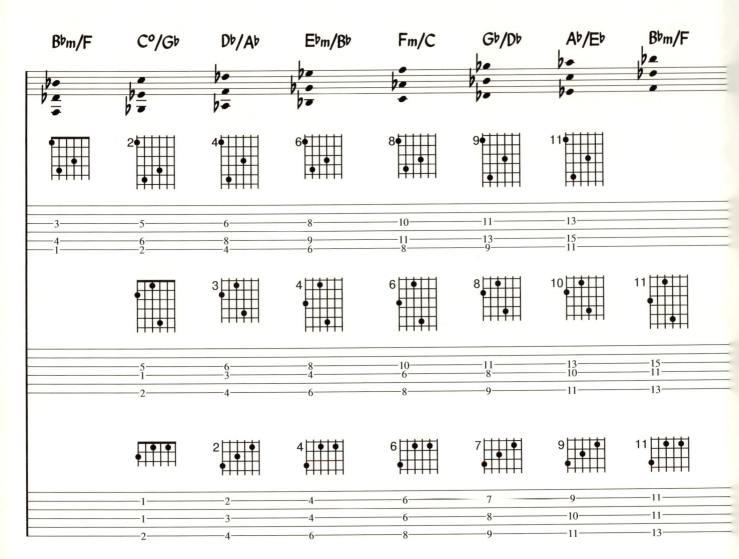

Root Position (open voiced, Version 2)

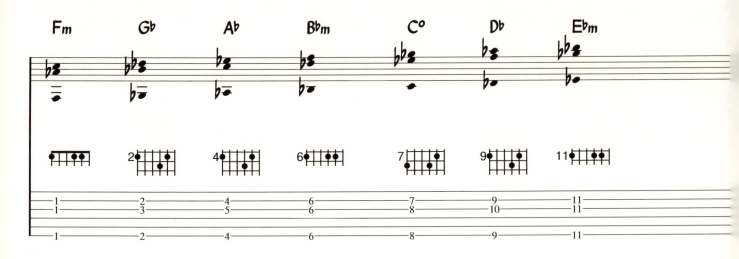

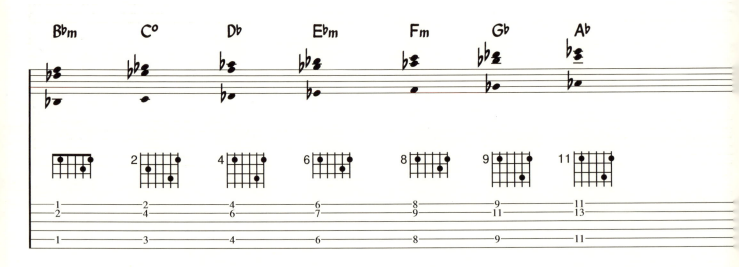

122

inv. (open voiced, Version 2)

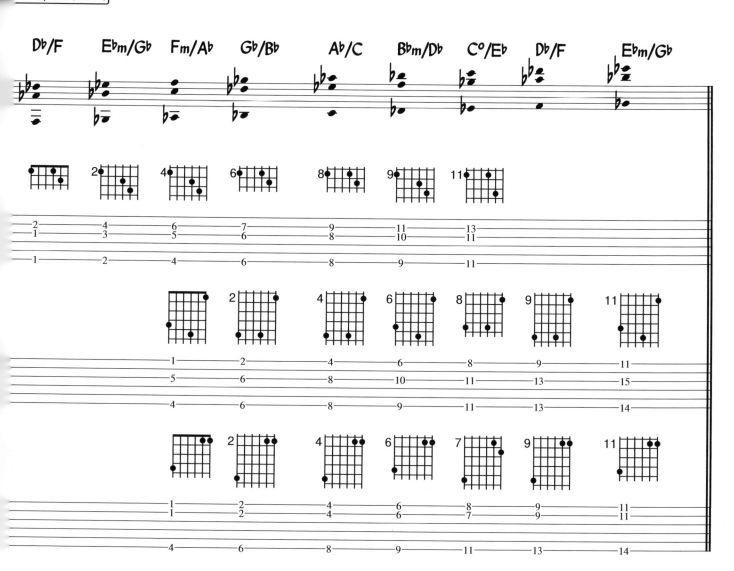
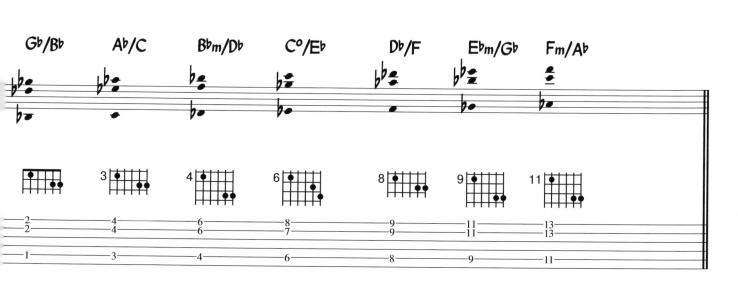

2nd inv. (open voiced, Version 2)

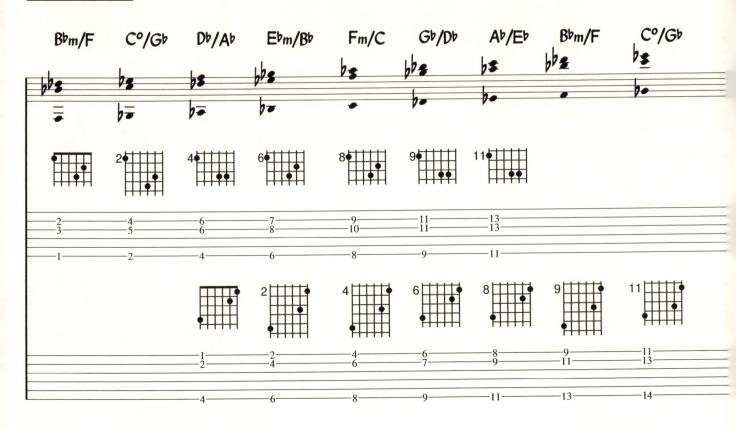
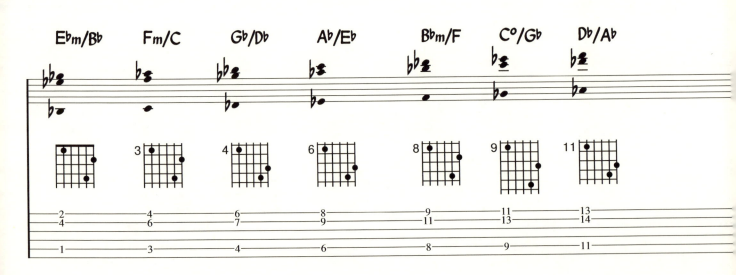

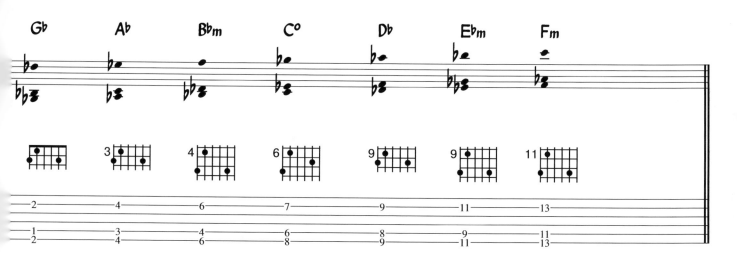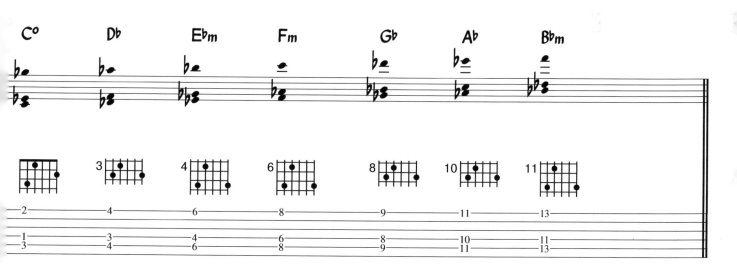

1st inv. (open voiced, Version 3)

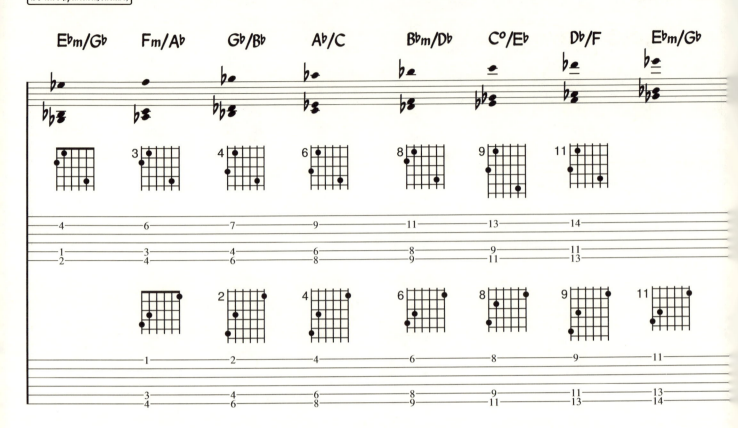
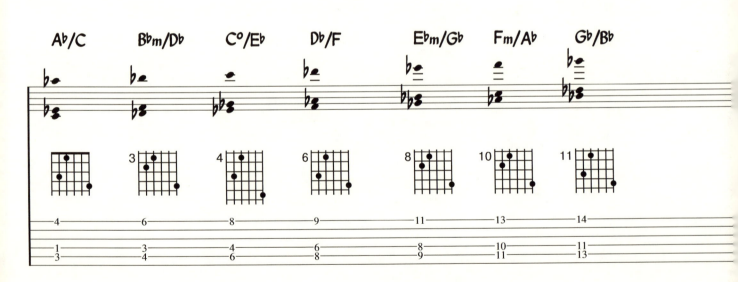

d inv. (open voiced, Version 3)

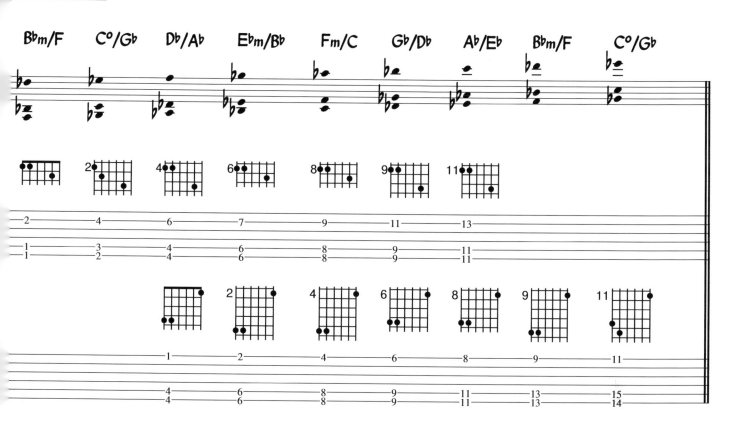
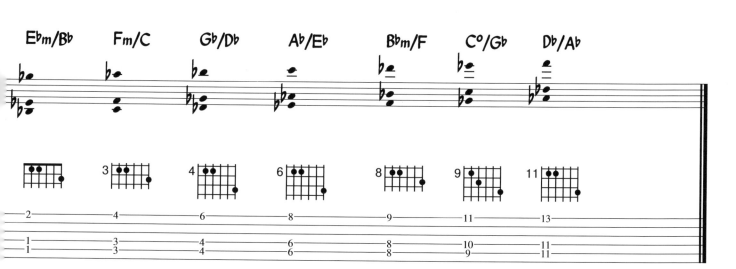

~ A♭ major ~

1st inv.

Root Position (open voiced)

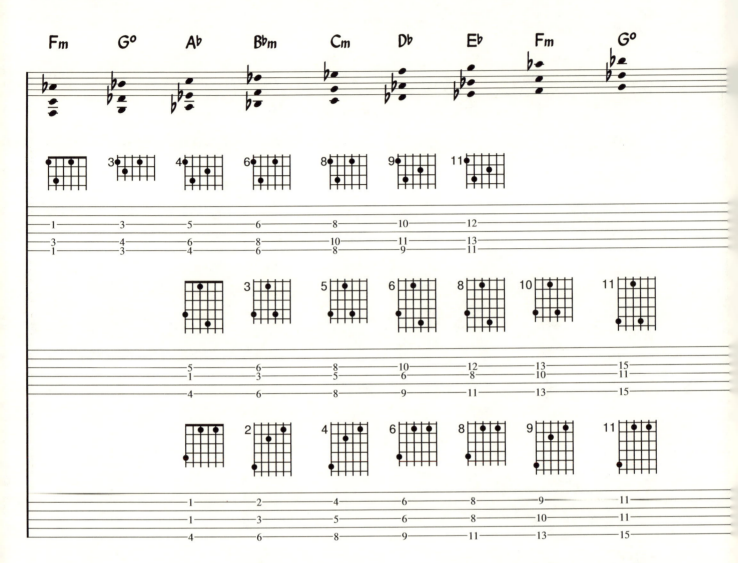

1st inv. (open voiced)

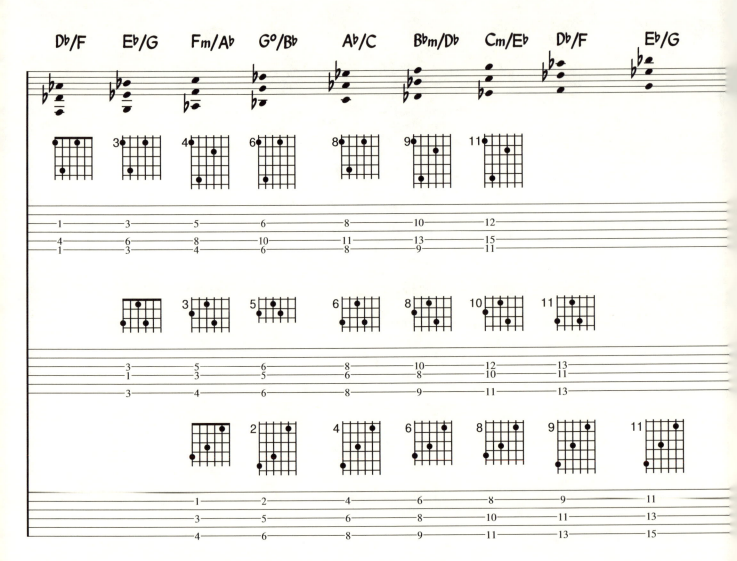

2nd inv. (open voiced)

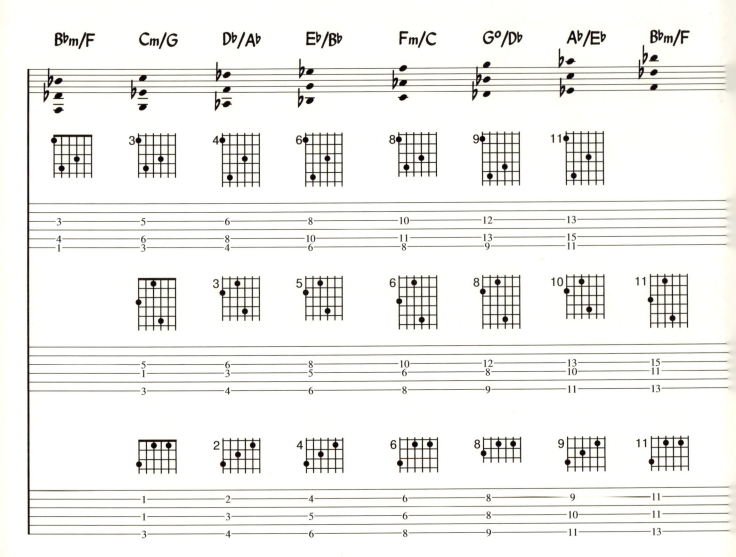

Root Position (open voiced, Version 2)

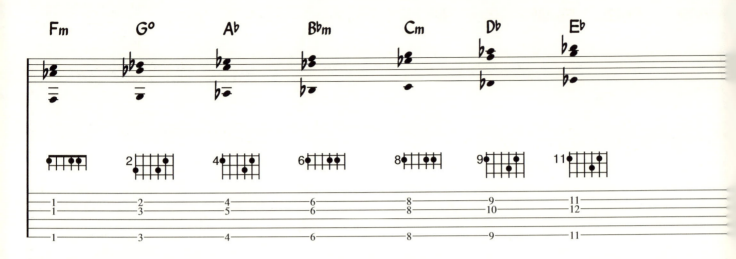

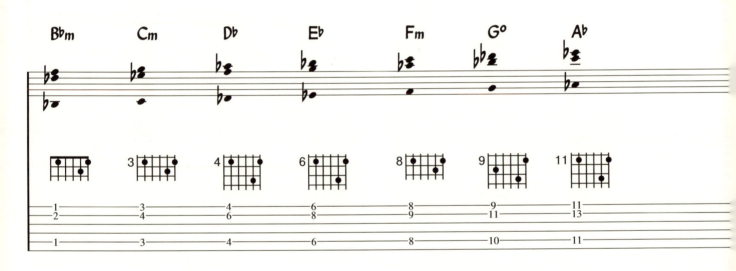

138

inv. (open voiced, Version 2)

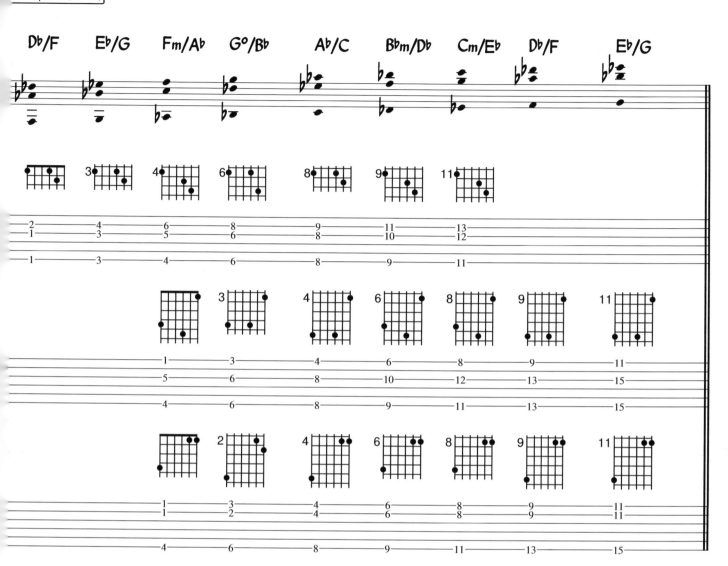
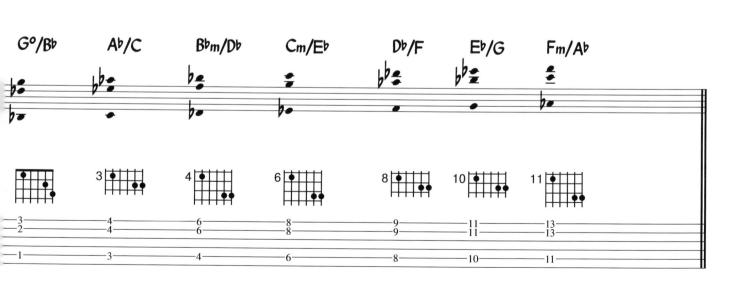

2nd inv. (open voiced, Version 2)

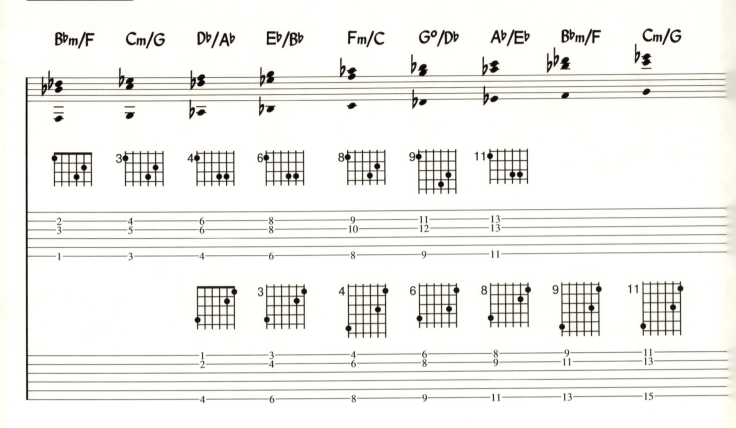
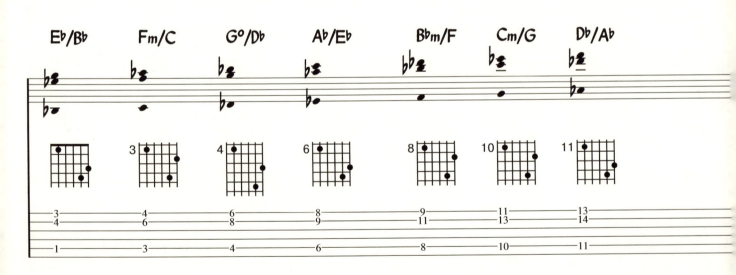

Root Position (open voiced, Version 3)

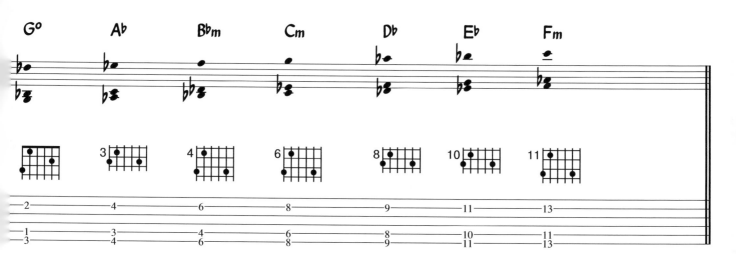
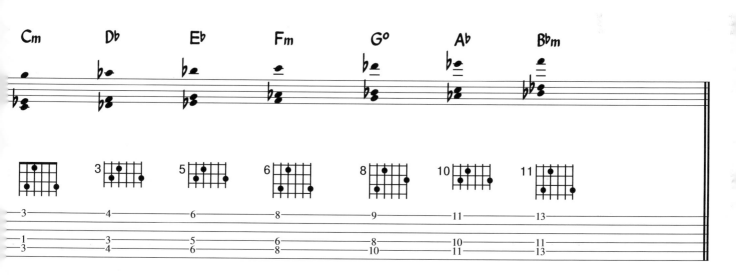

1st inv. (open voiced, Version 3)

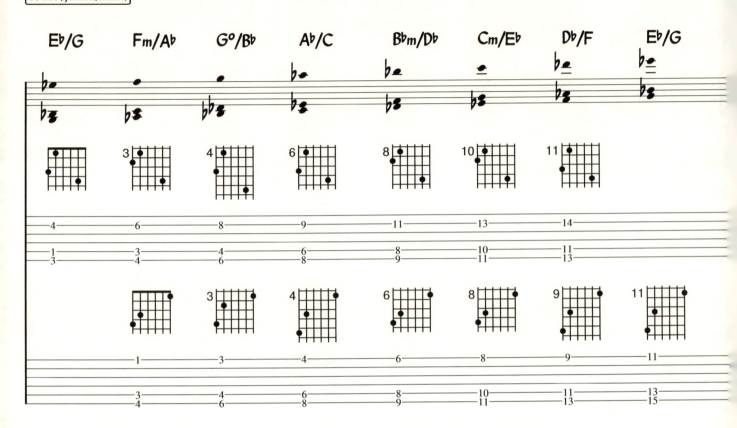

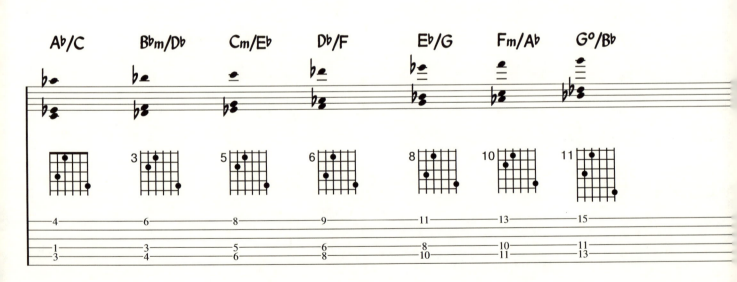

d inv. (open voiced, Version 3)

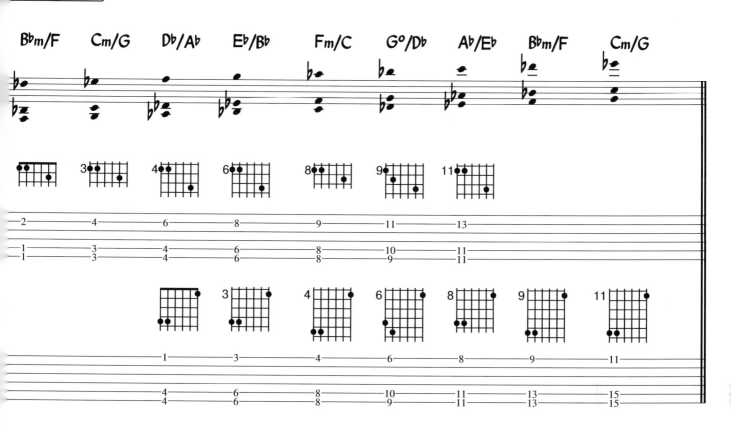

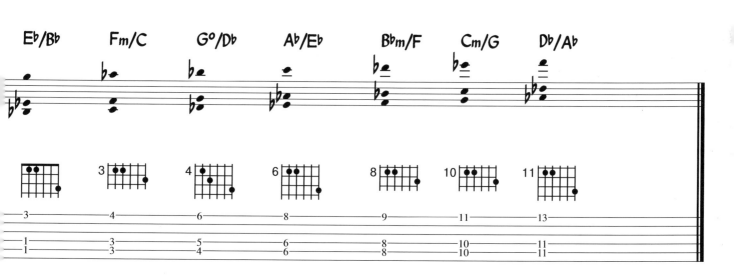

Root Position (open voiced)

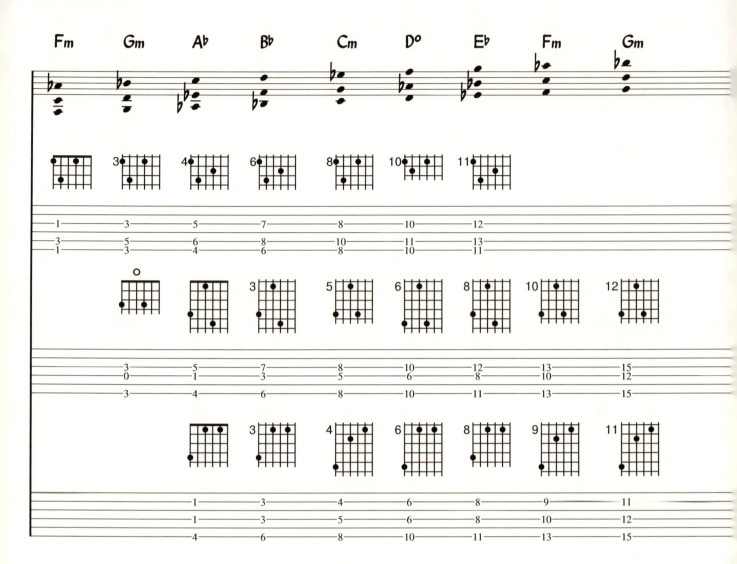

148

1st inv. (open voiced)

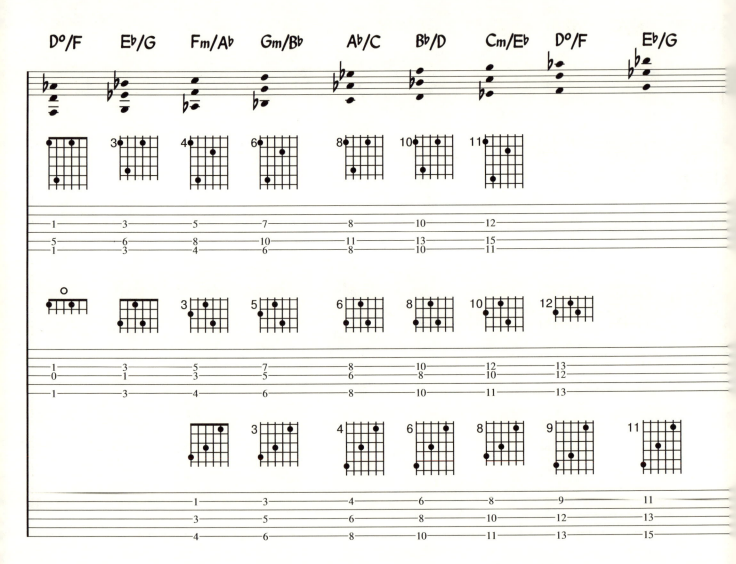

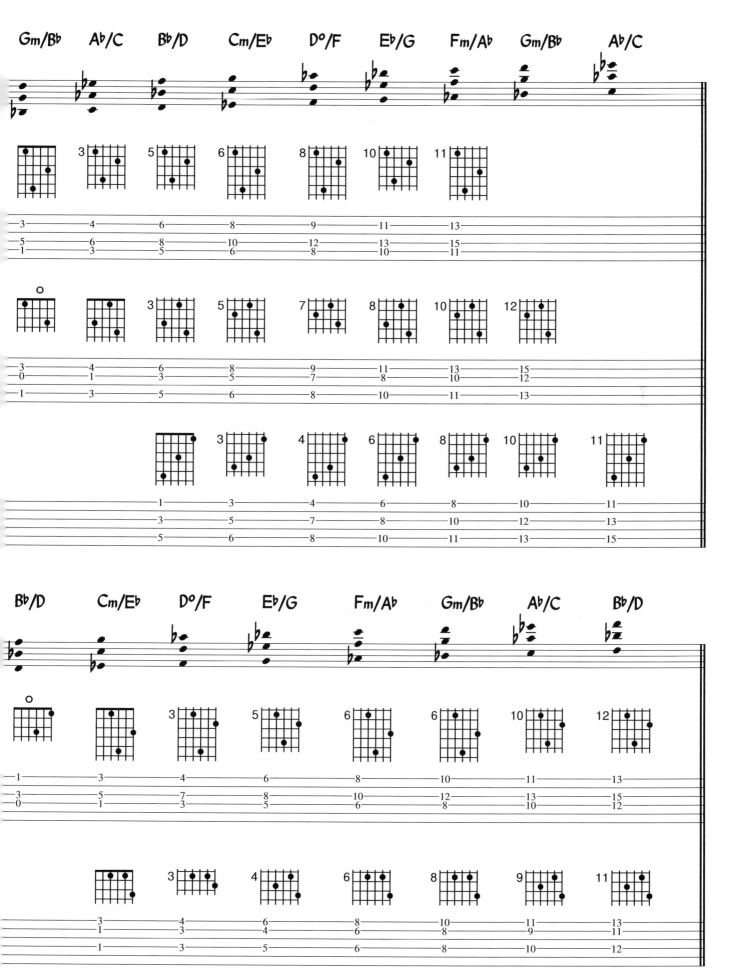

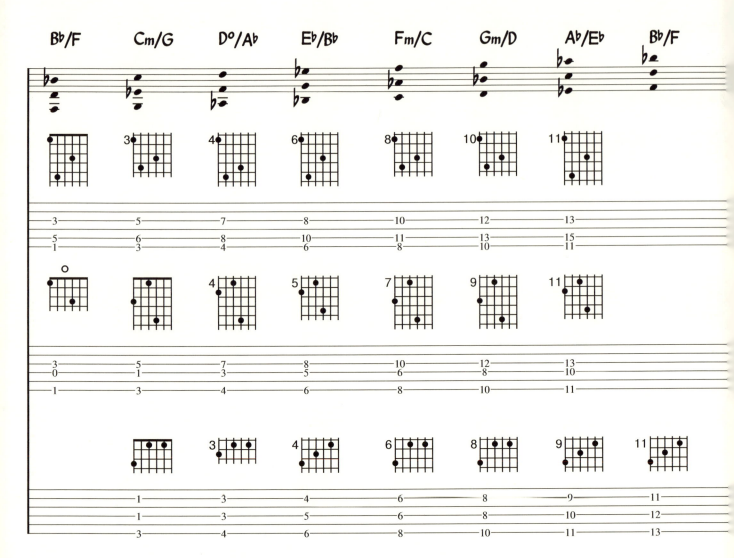

Root Position (open voiced, Version 2)

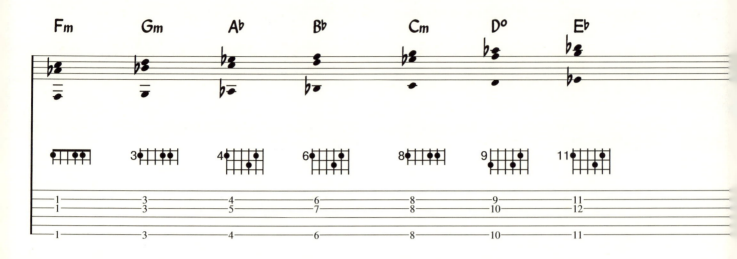

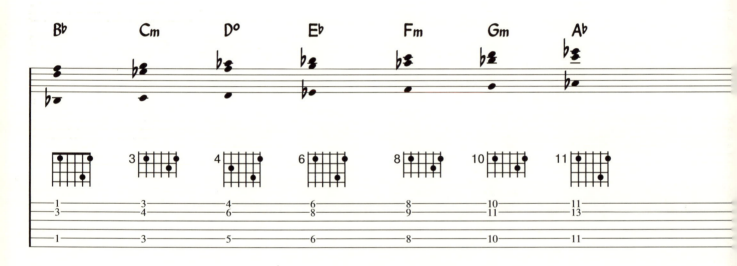

inv. (open voiced, Version 2)

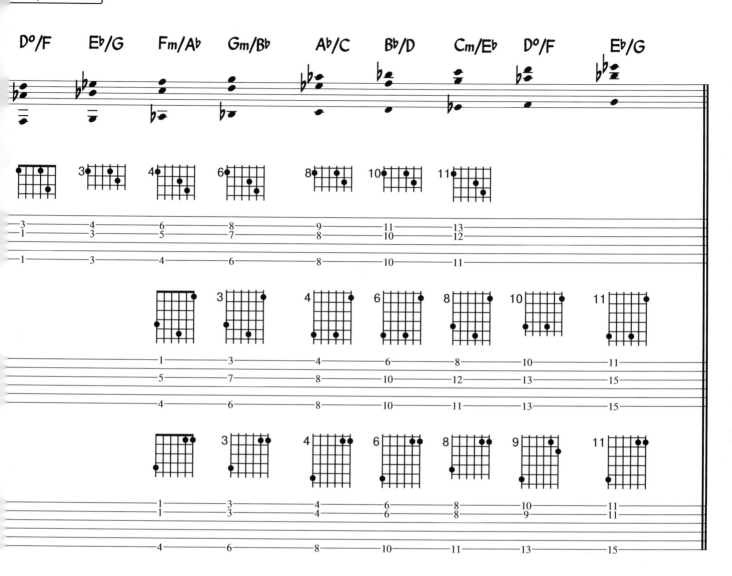
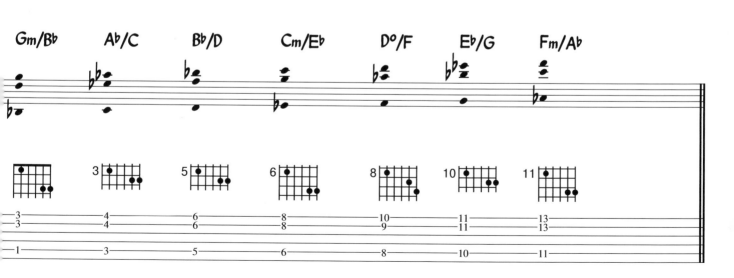

2nd inv. (open voiced, Version 2)

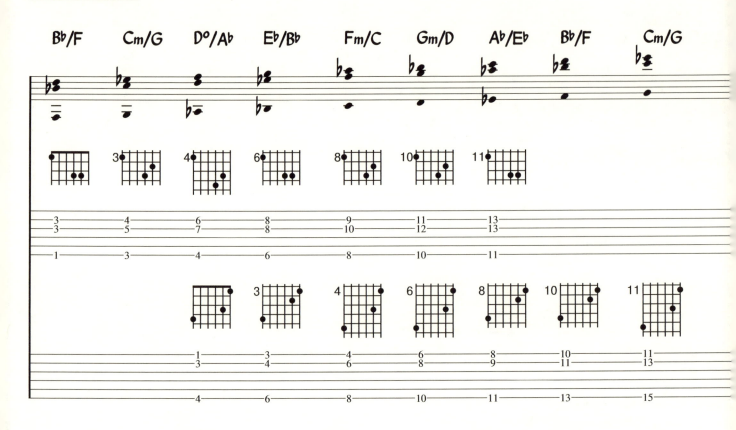
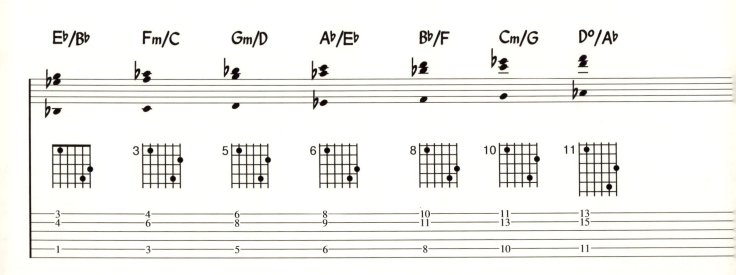

156

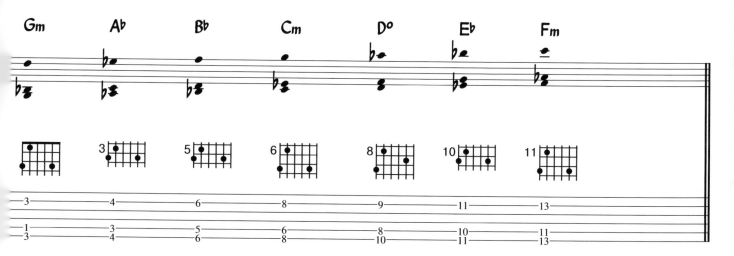
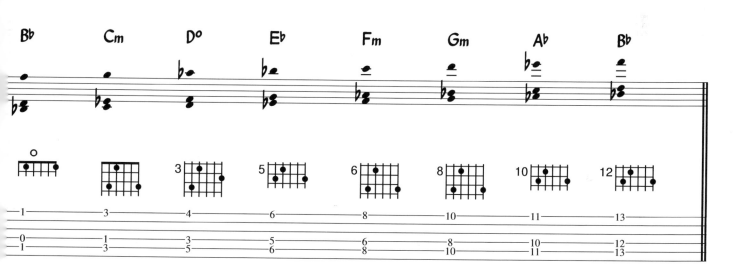

1st inv. (open voiced, Version 3)

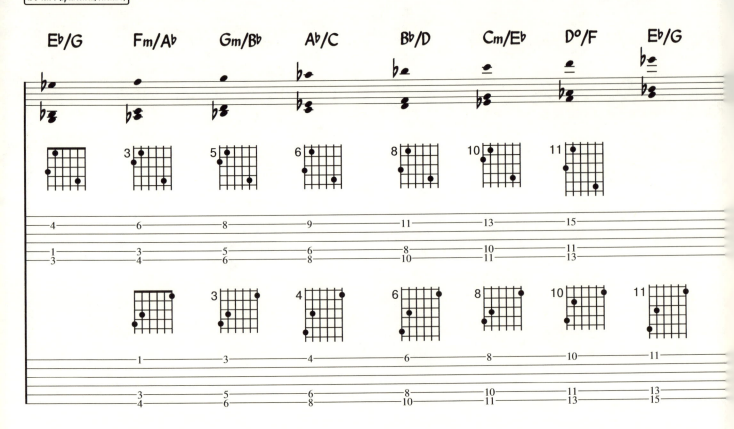
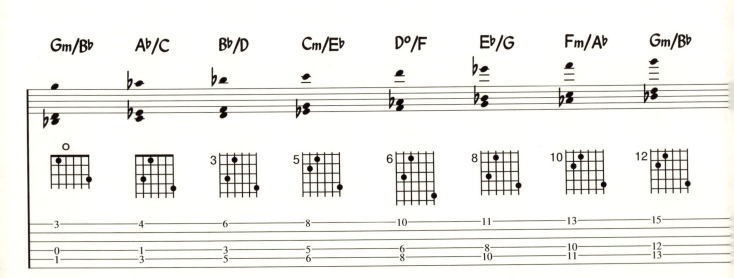

inv. (open voiced, Version 3)

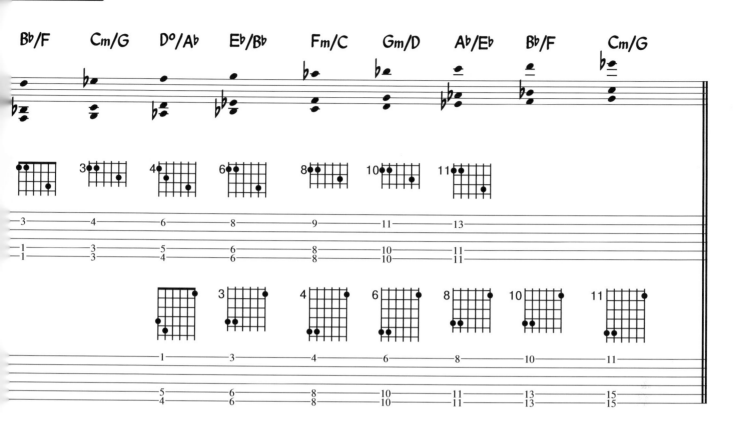
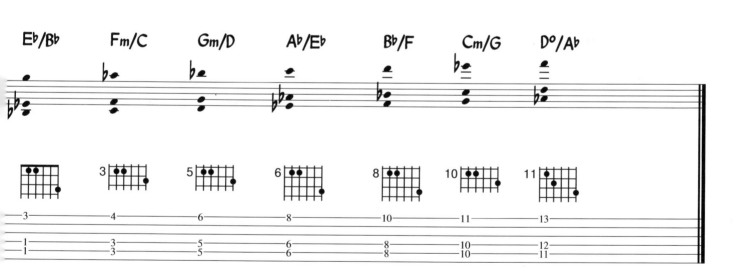

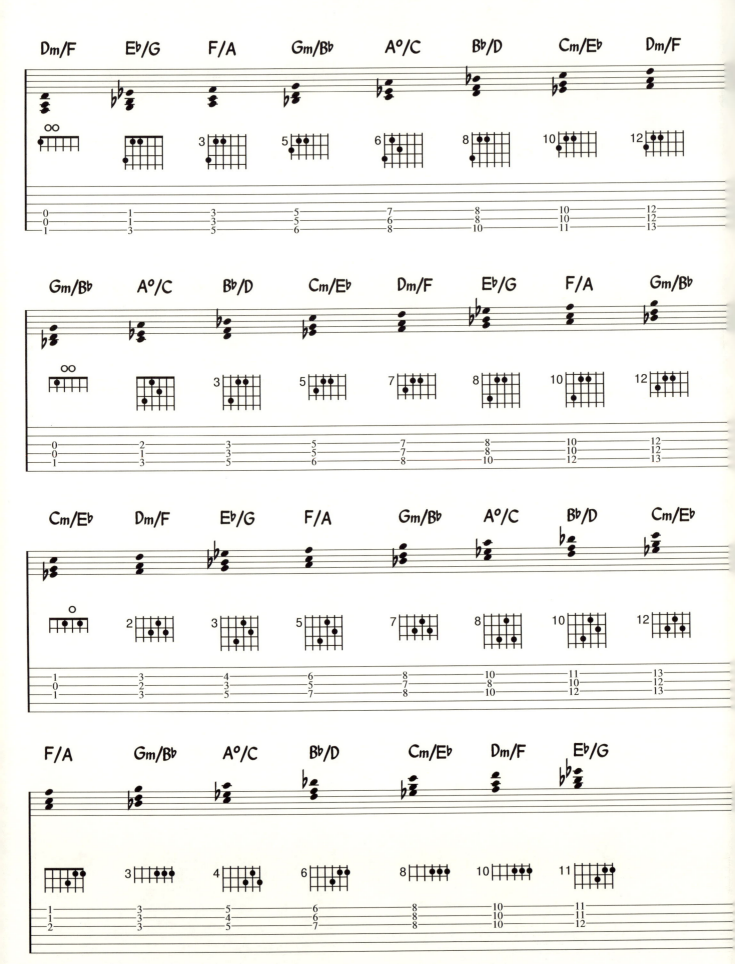

Root Position (open voiced)

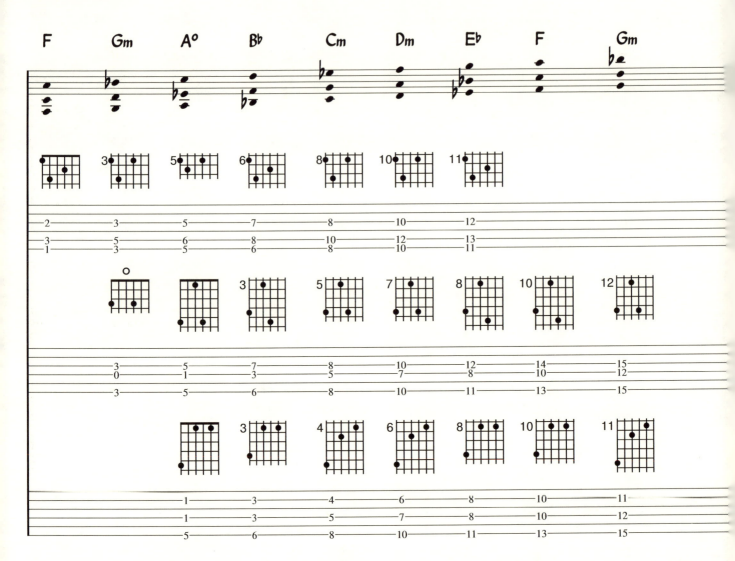

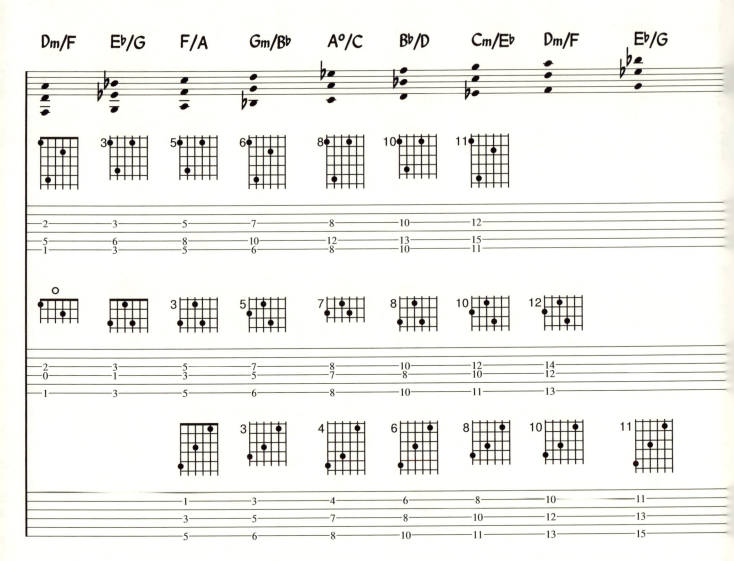

2nd inv. (open voiced)

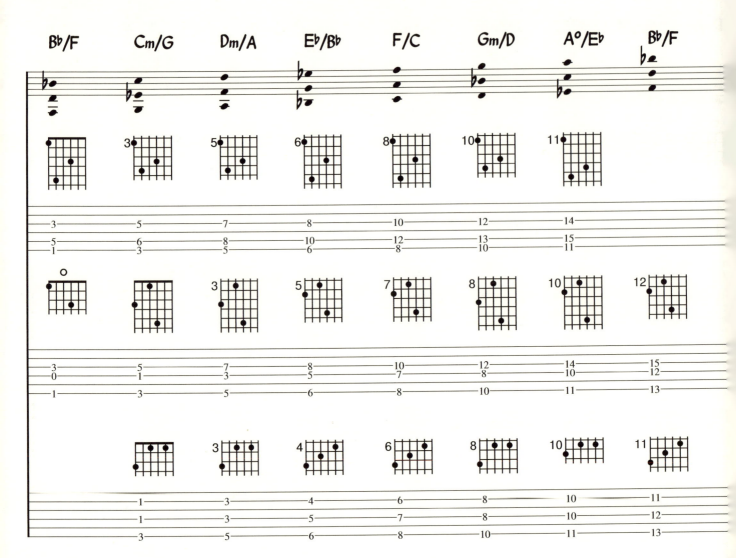

168

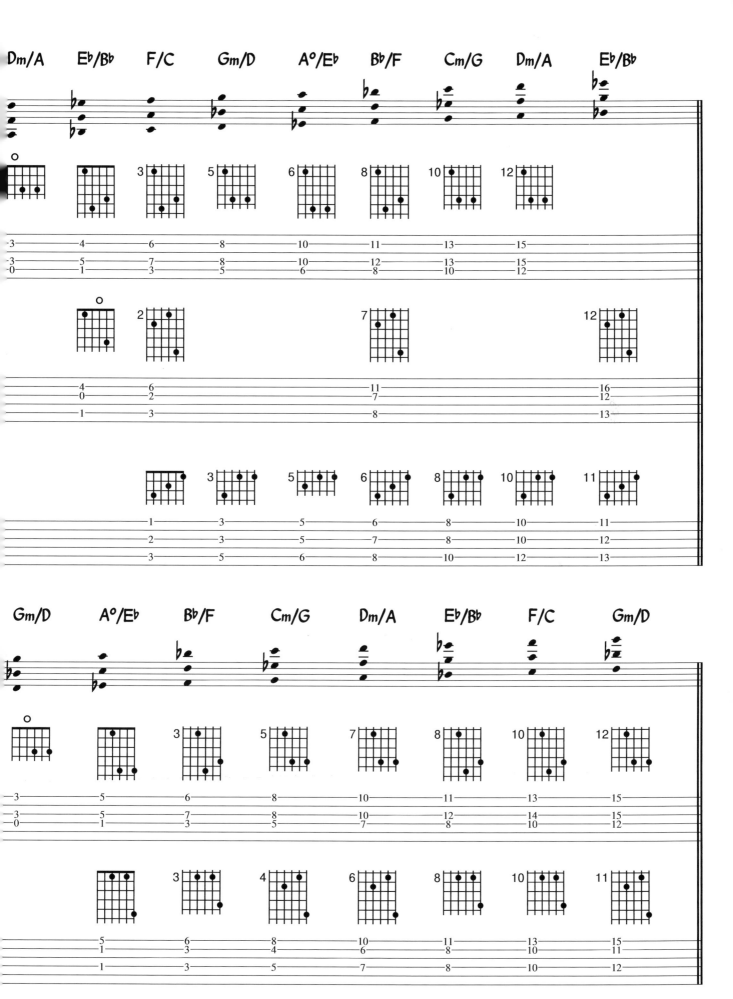

Root Position (open voiced, Version 2)

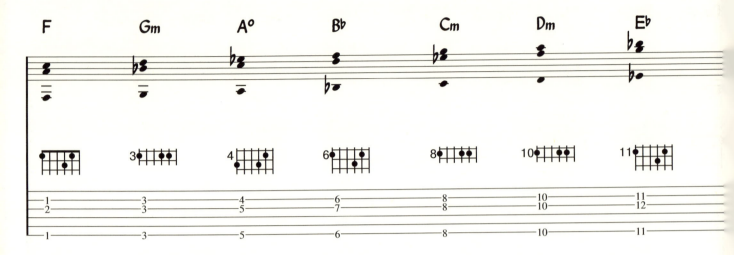

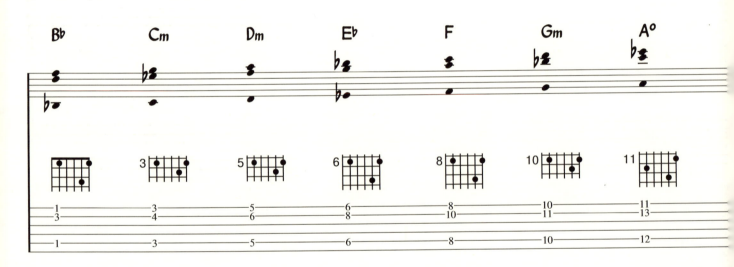

170

inv. (open voiced, Version 2)

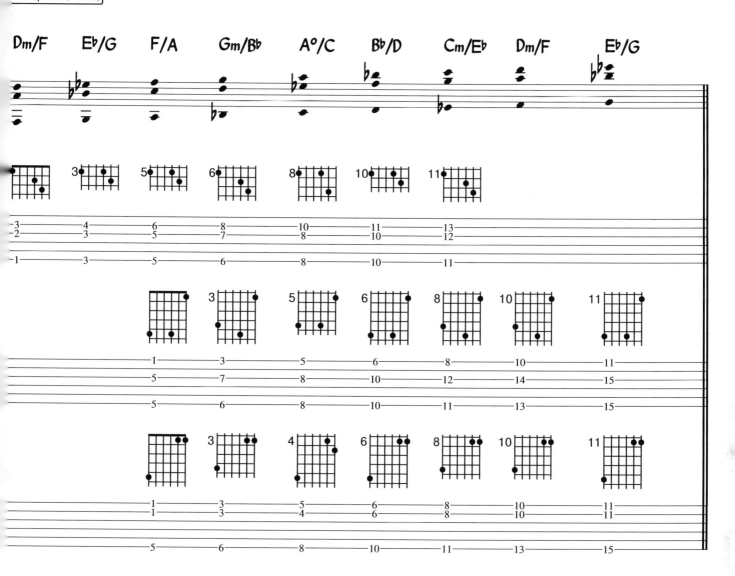
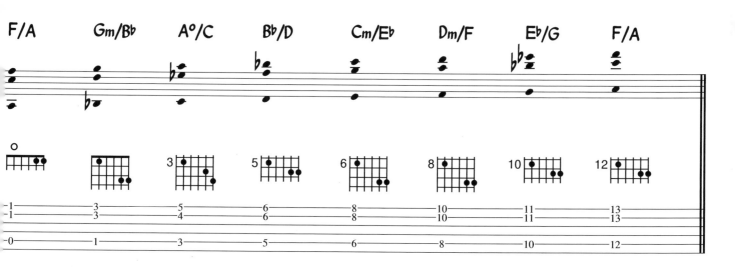

2nd inv. (open voiced, Version 2)

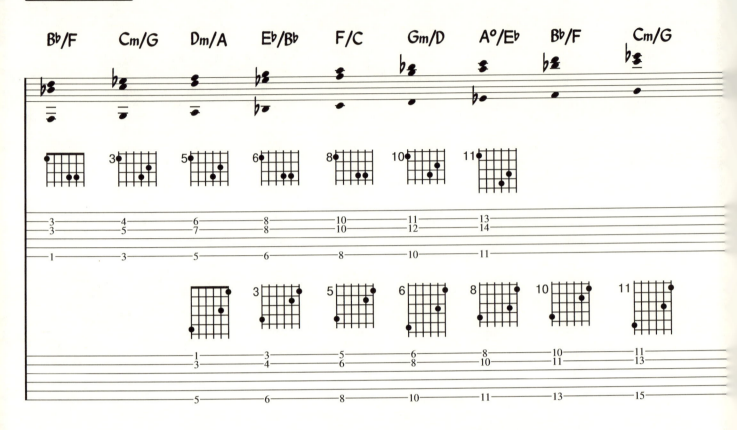
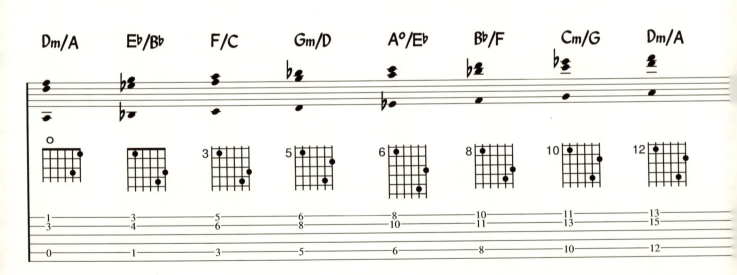

172

Root Position (open voiced, Version 3)

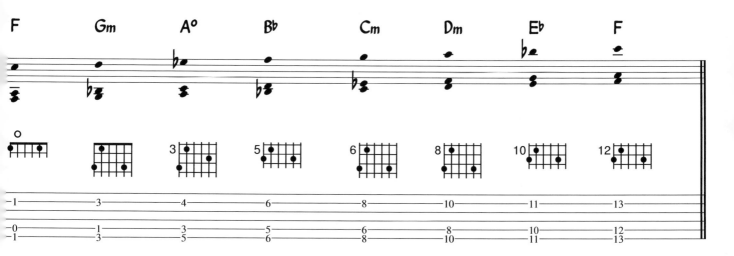

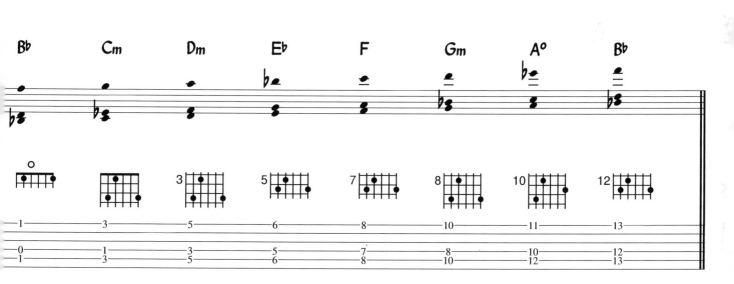

1st inv. (open voiced, Version 3)

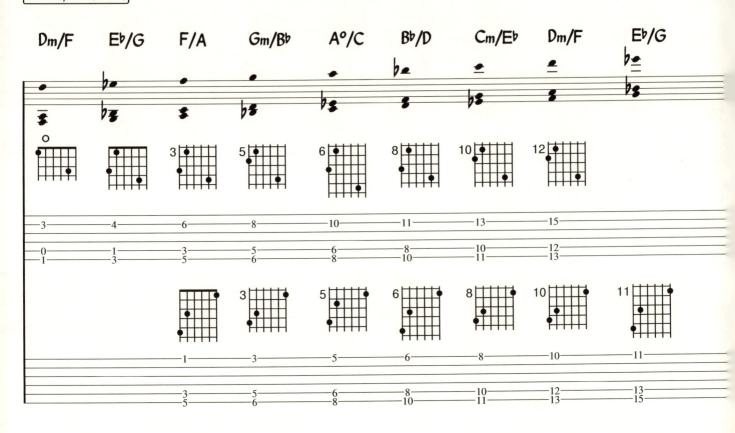
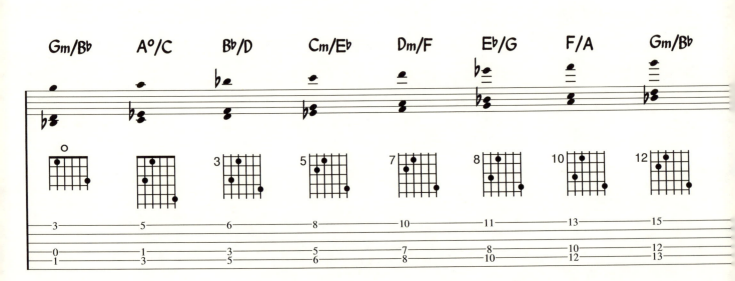

174

inv. (open voiced, Version 3)

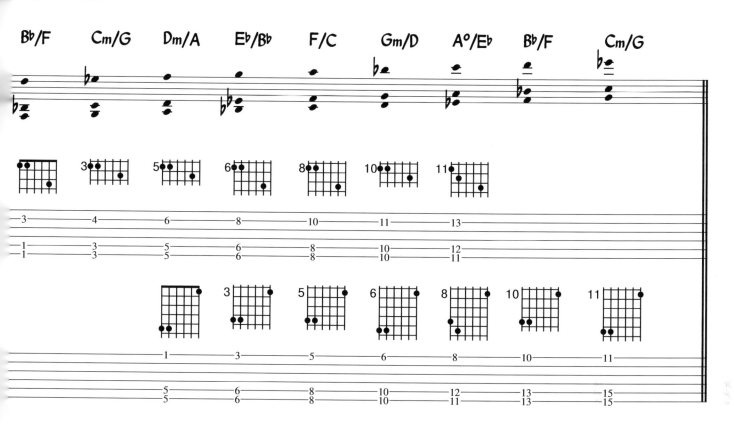
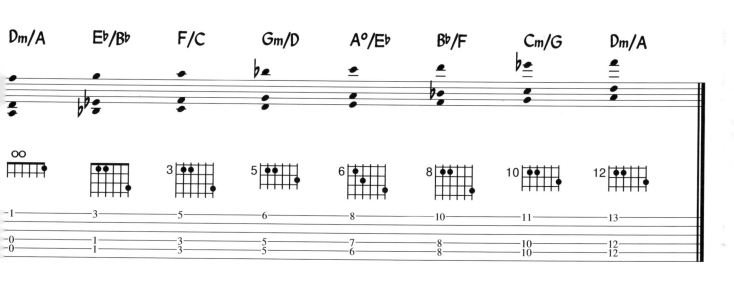

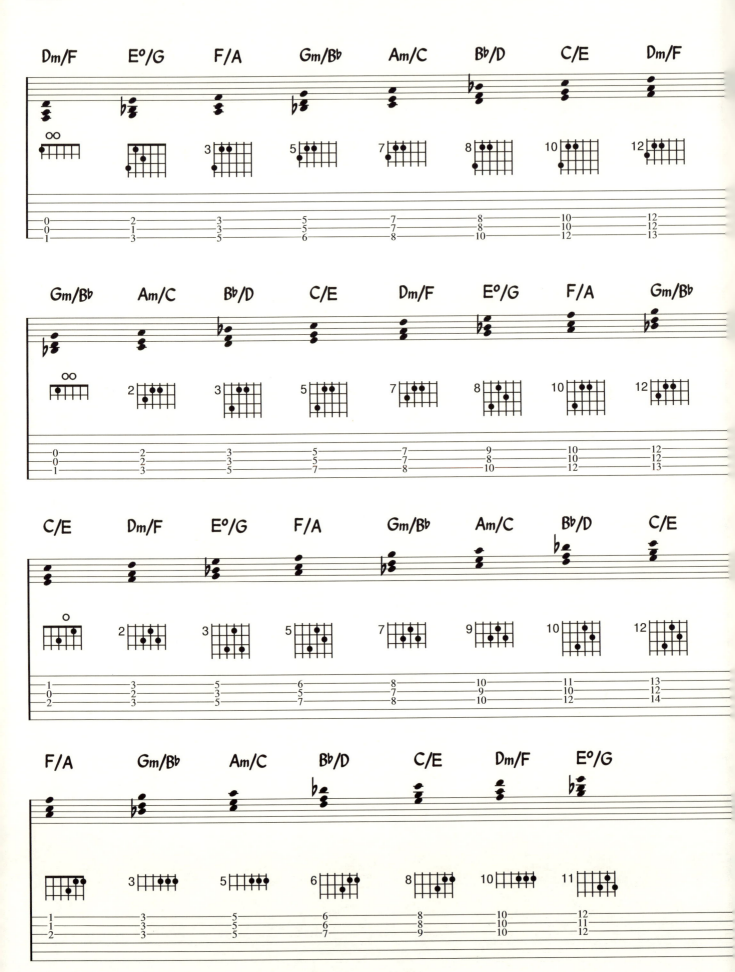

Root Position (open voiced)

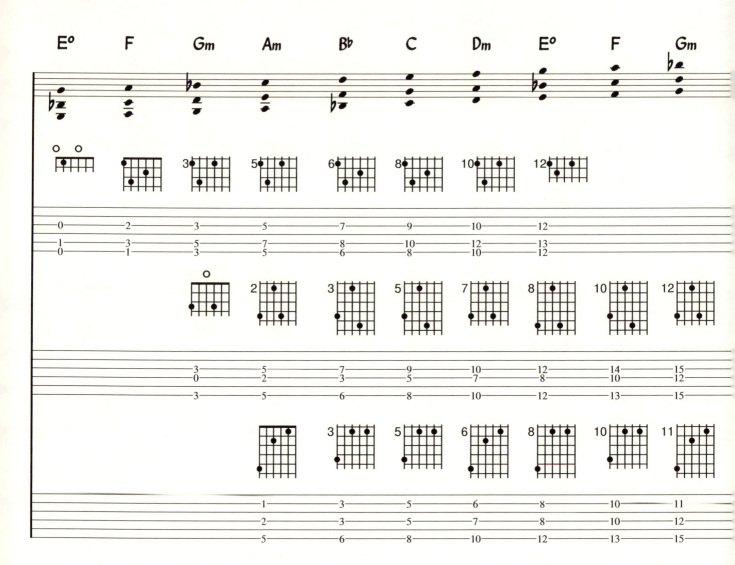

1st inv. (open voiced)

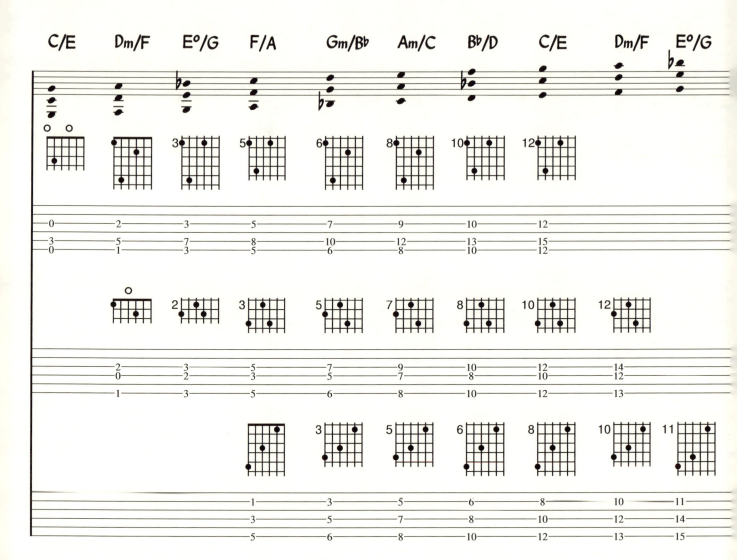

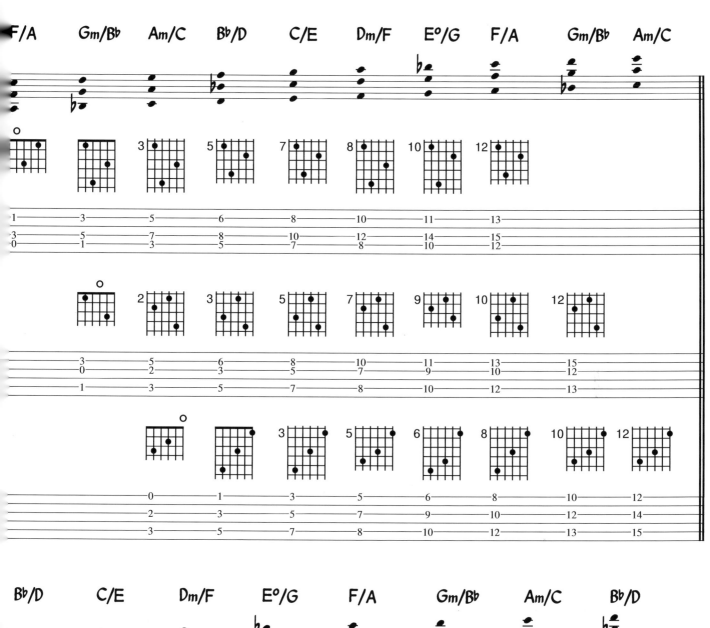
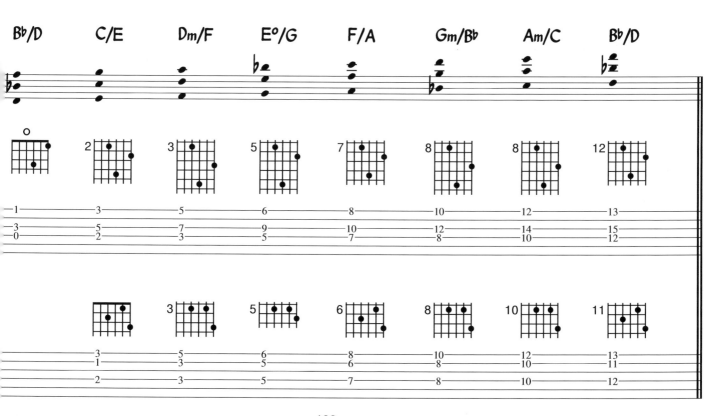

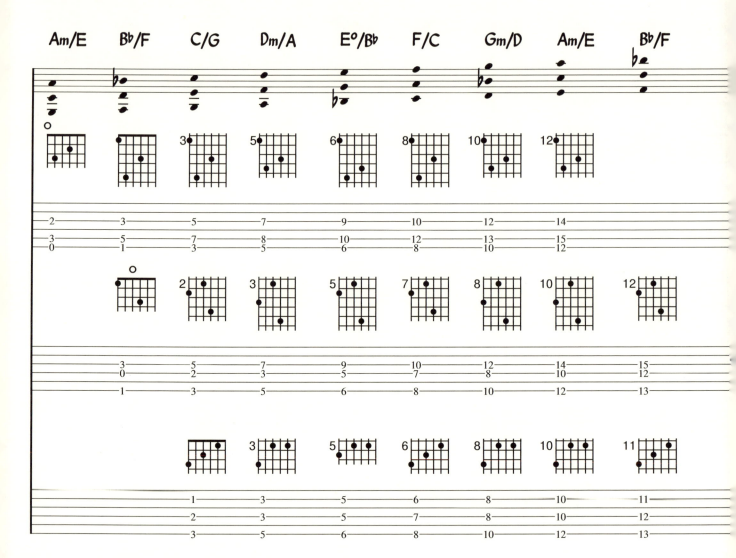

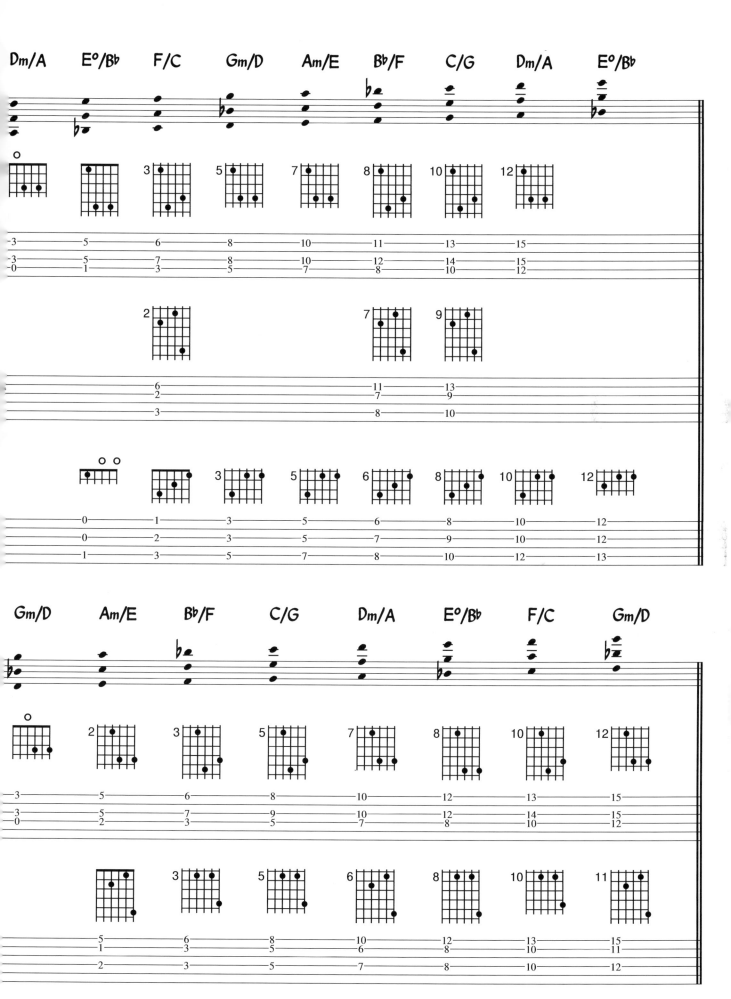

Root Position (open voiced, Version 2)

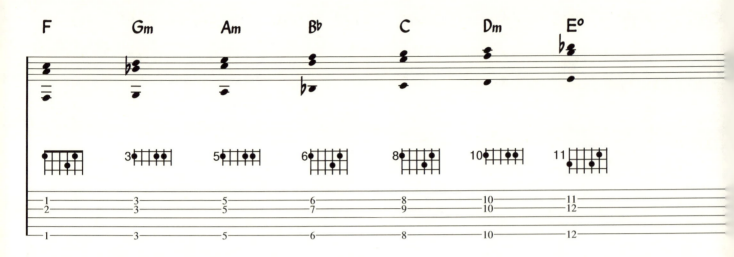
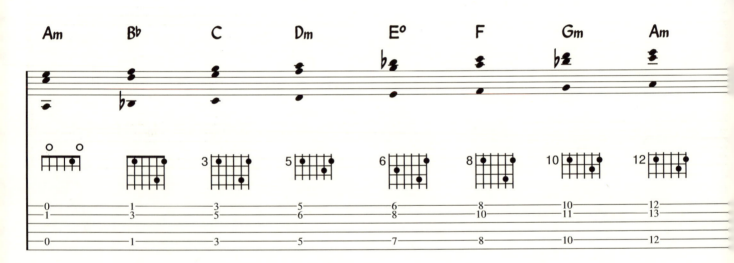

inv. (open voiced, Version 2)

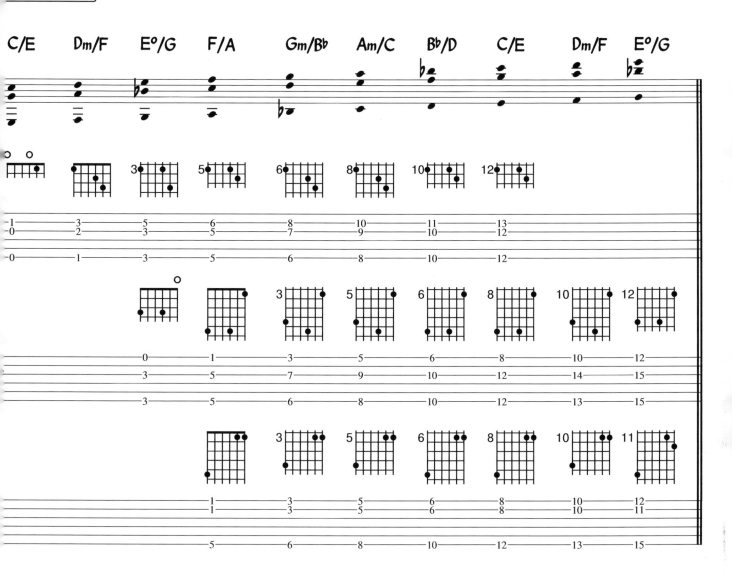
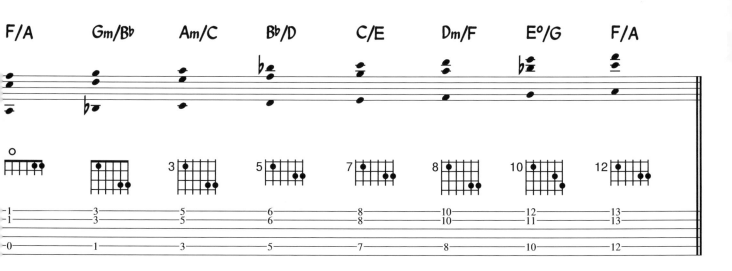

2nd inv. (open voiced, Version 2)

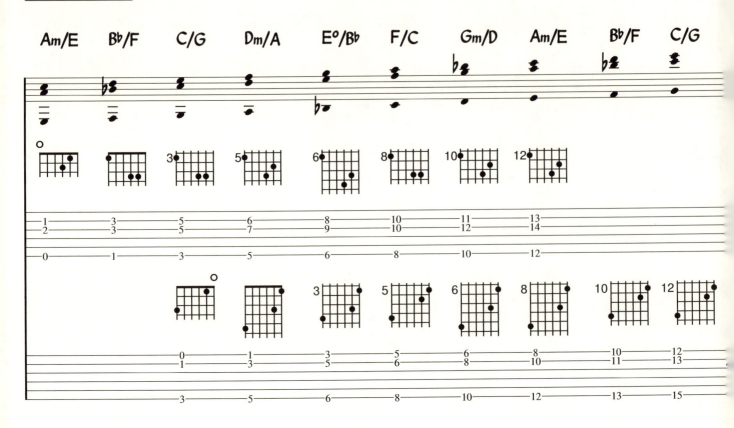
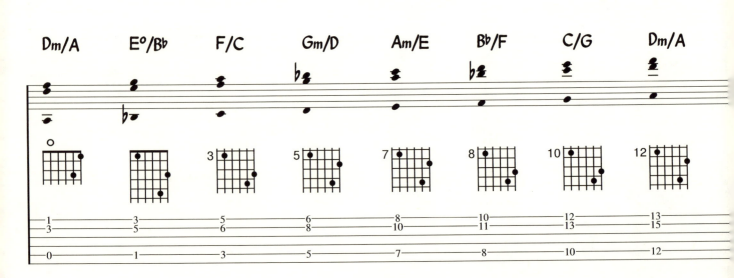

188

Root Position (open voiced, Version 3)

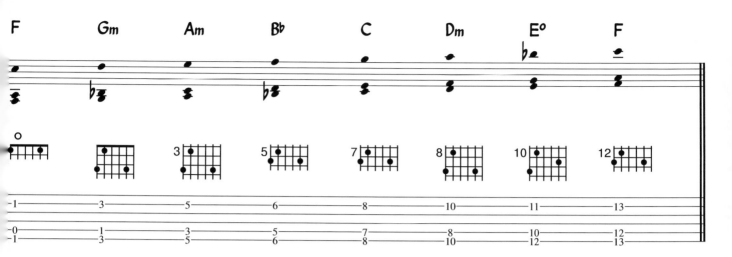
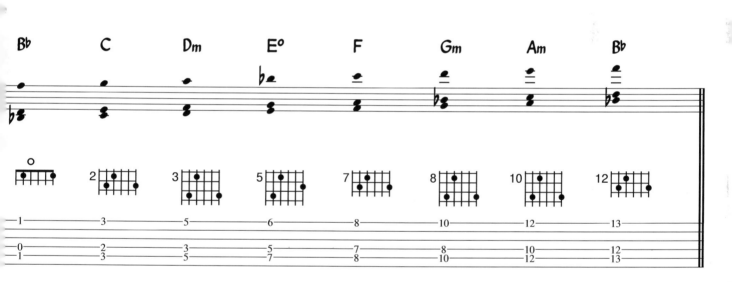

1st inv. (open voiced, Version 3)

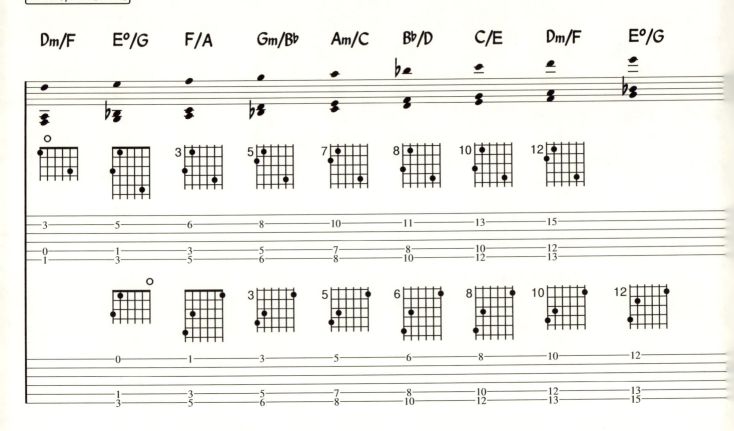
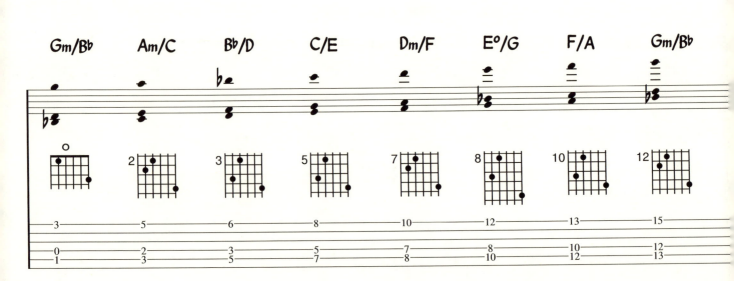

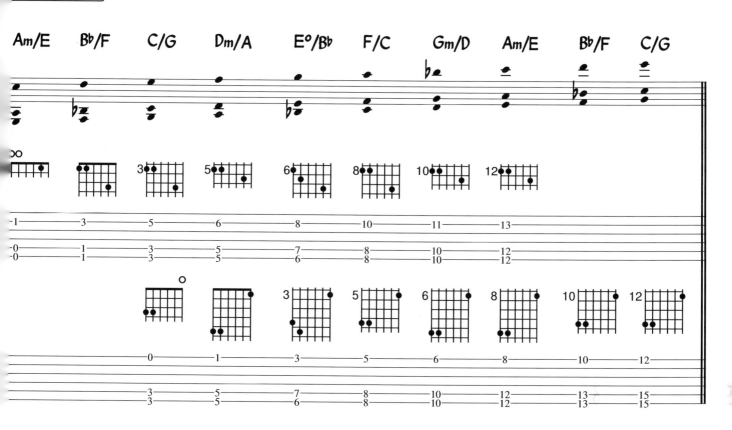
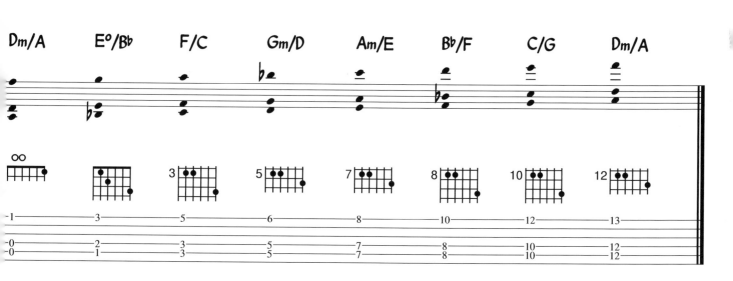

Made in the USA
Las Vegas, NV
22 February 2024